Unspoken lessons
about the unseen God

Unspoken lessons about the unseen God

Esther simply explained

Derek Prime

 EVANGELICAL PRESS

EVANGELICAL PRESS
Faverdale North Industrial Estate, Darlington, DL3 0PH, England

Evangelical Press USA
P. O. Box 84, Auburn, MA 01501, USA

e-mail: sales@evangelicalpress.org

web: http://www.evangelicalpress.org

First published 2001

British Library Cataloguing in Publication Data available

ISBN 0 85234 471 6

Printed and bound in Great Britain by Creative Print & Design Wales,
Ebbw Vale

Contents

Introduction

Esther is one of two Bible books named after a woman, Ruth being the other. Its position in the Old Testament, following Ezra and Nehemiah, is probably because of the role of Persia in all three books. The background to Esther is a plan to exterminate the Jewish people throughout the Persian Empire, a recurring theme in world history and, sadly, all too contemporary.

A unique feature

Perhaps what people remember most about the book of Esther is that it is one of two books in the Bible where God's name is not mentioned. The other is the Song of Solomon. Whereas, in its 167 verses, the Persian king is mentioned 190 times, no explicit reference is made to God.

Although the name of God (Yahweh) is not mentioned in Esther, some Hebrew scholars have found this name repeated four times in the Hebrew text in acrostic form, as a kind of code to the discerning reader. Others have discovered anagrams of God's name in three passages, and yet others have claimed to find abbreviations of it within the Hebrew text.

Too much must not be made of such features, however, as they remain a matter of speculation.

Paradoxical as it may seem, however, the book's main lessons are about God. The writer deliberately avoids using God's name, but reckons upon his involvement at every stage of the narrative.

Various reasons have been suggested for the absence of God's name. First, and perhaps the most obvious, yet frequently overlooked, is that *it is intentional*, since its omission teaches the fundamental lesson that when God seems most absent in human affairs, he may be most present and at work. Jews who read the history of Esther thoughtfully were reminded of Joseph. Earlier in their history he had declared to his brothers, 'You intended to harm me, but God intended it for good to accomplish what is now being done, the saving of many lives.'[1] The book of Esther provides the same assurance.

Secondly, *God's displeasure with his people* may be expressed by his seeming absence and silence. Deuteronomy 31:18 suggests this possibility: 'And I will certainly hide my face on that day because of all their wickedness in turning to other gods.'[2] If that truth applies here, God was hiding his face from his people on account of their sins. Many had deliberately chosen to remain in the land of their captivity among the heathen, instead of returning to Jerusalem under Zerubbabel as others had done.[3]

Third, it has been suggested that the name of God is absent because of *the author's fear of Persian censorship* of his book. In a similar way, both Peter and John do not mention Rome by name but employ substitutes.[4]

Fourth, the book of Esther is intended to be read annually by Jews on the Day of Purim, a day of feasting (9:19,22). It is celebrated on the 14th of Adar (end of February and the beginning of March), the twelfth month of the Babylonian lunar calendar used by the Jews after the exile.[5] It is the only holiday in the Jewish calendar that is light-hearted, although serious in its record of a momentous event. The Jewish Mishnah (an important collection of codes and laws, forming the first section of the Talmud, a collection of Jewish writings of the early Christian centuries) lays down the rule that on this feast the people are to drink until they are unable to distinguish between 'Blessed be Mordecai!' and 'Cursed be Haman!' The danger of such feasting is excessive drinking and careless speech in which *God's name might be used lightly or treated with irreverence*. But this is the least likely explanation.

However, although God is not mentioned, his overruling providence is the background to all the proceedings described in the book. It shows that we cannot tell what God may be doing at the time in history that events happen. The book is remarkable for its number of 'coincidences', as, for example, in the timing of the king's calling for the reading of the chronicles of his reign (6:1), or of Haman's entry into the court just at the very time when Xerxes was wondering how to reward Mordecai (6:4), or the moment when the king returned to find Haman in the act of falling upon Esther's couch (7:8).

God's providence is especially alluded to in Esther 4:14. Mordecai was confident that his people's salvation would come from an unidentified source, whatever Esther's response to his request. He knew God had a purpose in having enabled the Jews to survive in Persia. Fasting — the accompaniment of prayer to God — is also mentioned in 4:16 and 9:31. The book encourages us in a greater trust in God's providence, a providence that is universal, national and personal to each of us.

When and where?

The events recorded in the book of Esther took place in the Persian Empire in the fifth century B.C. It is the only Old

Testament book in which the entire narrative takes place in Persia. Throughout the fifth century, the Persians ruled Palestine. Esther, Daniel, Ezra, Nehemiah and 2 Chronicles 36:22-23 all relate to this period. The book of Esther helps to fill the gap between chapters 6 and 7 of the book of Ezra. Like Ezra, Nehemiah and Daniel, it shows us how Jews behaved, or were forced to behave, in exile.

The Persians created the greatest empire of ancient times before that of Rome, and they sustained it for two centuries. It was one of several (i.e. Babylonian, Greek and Roman) that ruled Palestine over a period of 650 years. Persia conquered Babylonia in 539 B.C. (nearly sixty years after the Jews were exiled there). Of all the conquerors of the Jews, the Persians stand out as the least evil and hostile towards them. A decree of Cyrus in 539 B.C. permitted Jews held captive in Babylon to return to Jerusalem, but relatively few availed themselves of the opportunity, preferring to remain where they had settled, and some — as the book of Esther demonstrates — rose to positions of importance.

The principal characters

The principal characters are Xerxes, Haman, Esther and Mordecai. Xerxes is the Greek form of the Hebrew Ahasuerus. Just as in Egypt the common name for the king was Pharaoh, in Persia it was Ahasuerus. Haman was his adviser and the villain of the story. Esther and Mordecai were Jews who put their confidence in God in desperate circumstances.

These individuals are worthy of study in themselves in view of the different aspects of human character they display. Xerxes was a bunch of contradictions. He was authoritarian and impulsive, yet ready to yield to counsel and to protect those who had been wronged.

Haman is as prominent as the king, and we are given particular insight into his emotions[6] and thoughts.[7] He represents ethnic prejudice — a problem common in our contemporary world. He compels us to face up to the perils of racism and ethnic conflict. He stands out as proud, self-seeking and spiteful. He takes for granted his ability to be the master of his own destiny, although when in danger he is a coward and weak. His story needs to be read in the light of passages such as Psalm 37:32-36:

> The wicked lie in wait for the righteous,
>   seeking their very lives;
> but the LORD will not leave them in their power
>   or let them be condemned when brought to trial.
> Wait for the LORD
>   and keep his way.
> He will exalt you to inherit the land;
>   when the wicked are cut off, you will see it.
> I have seen a wicked and ruthless man
>   flourishing like a green tree in its native soil,
> but he soon passed away and was no more;
>   though I looked for him, he could not be found.

Haman is a classic example of poetic justice, or of someone hoist with his own petard, in that what happens to him in the end is exactly what he deserved.

Esther, on the other hand, stands out as humble, self-effacing, patient and practical in her wisdom. Although it is not spelt out, her faith in God becomes evident, and it provides her with courage to do what is demanded of her. In her relationship to Mordecai, she shows herself grateful and obedient. Given the position of a queen, she rises to the responsibility and uses her initiative for the good of others, and especially her own people.

Mordecai exhibits a true fear of God, putting it before the fear of man. He does his duty without seeking reward. Raised to prominence, he shows generosity, justice and mercy. Although exiled, he had not lost his sense of identity as a Jew (2:5-6). No matter what the pressures were to compromise, he determined to keep God's law (3:2-4) and trust God (4:15-17).

Lesser characters are also deserving of attention. Vashti is not described in detail, but she exhibits courage, dignity and resolution. Haman's wife, Zeresh, illustrates the danger of automatically siding with one's marriage partner without endeavouring to provide a corrective when that partner's judgement and behaviour are plainly wrong and dangerous.

Principles of right behaviour are often best understood by examples. The Wisdom Literature of the Old Testament finds superb illustration in the character and actions of Esther and Mordecai, who display the wisdom God gives, in contrast to Xerxes and Haman, who display foolishness, the unspiritual wisdom Satan promotes. The whole book illustrates the wisdom which the book of Proverbs strives to impress upon us. It is not without significance that we shall find ourselves referring to that book more than any other.

The main lessons

The four principal lessons are about God: his preservation of his people, the mysteries, yet certainty, of his providence, the severity of his judgement and the importance of remembering his past mercies.

Besides these principal lessons there are others of importance: the perils of anti-Semitism; the utilizing of God-given opportunities; the harmony of human responsibility and divine providence; the dangers of pride and the blessings of trust in

God; and the choice we all have to make as to whether we are going to belong to God's people or his enemies. The book demonstrates how God chooses 'the foolish things of the world to shame the wise' and 'the weak things of the world to shame the strong'.[8] History has had its Hamans, and this book encourages us to believe that they will all be brought low.

A crisis manual

The book of Esther had particular significance for Jews of the Dispersion, or Diaspora, the name given to Jews living outside of Palestine. It is outstanding for the answers it gives to God's people in exile, and we may describe it as 'a crisis manual for God's people'. Esther's position as a woman and orphan symbolized the precarious situation of many Jews scattered throughout the then-known world. The book provides answers to key and burning issues such as: 'Where should God's people look for God when they are away from their own land? How can they best survive and prosper when scattered among the nations? What should their attitude be to non-Jewish states and governments? How should they behave in times of crisis? How should they function as a community in exile?' It provides an alternative to the book of Daniel as a model for Jewish life in time of exile.

The identity of the author and the date of writing

The author's name is unknown. The book is written anonymously. Josephus (*c*. 37 – 100), a Jewish historian, considered Mordecai to be the author,[9] as did Clement of Alexandria (*c*.155 – *c*. 220) on account of 9:20-32. Not a few ancient Jewish and Christian scholars have followed the same line of thought. Mordecai has been, and probably remains, the most favoured candidate, although there are indications in the book that militate against this suggestion, such as the description of his prominence in 10:3. Augustine (354 – 430) thought the writer was Ezra, and the Talmud ascribes it to the members of the great synagogue established by Ezra and Nehemiah. The truth remains that we do not know the identity of the author.

Much debate also surrounds the date of the writing of the book. Our inability to identify the author makes our determining the date of its composition all the more difficult. The author certainly wrote as if the period when Xerxes was king had been some long time ago.[10] He seems to have had access to some of Mordecai's writings (9:20) and 'the book of the annals of the kings of Media and Persia' (2:23; 10:2), and to have written before the Persian Empire fell to Greece in 330 B.C. He was undoubtedly a Jew living in Persia, probably writing in the middle of the fourth century B.C., and not later than 350 B.C. However, the date remains an open question, with no clues really provided in the text.

Whatever the author's identity, and the time of writing, he possessed an intimate knowledge of Persia and the Persians. He provides, for example, a great deal of information about the king's palace, with his mention of 'the king's gate' (2:19), an 'outer court' (6:4), as well as an 'inner court' (4:11) and a harem (2:9), with different parts (2:14) and its own courtyard (2:11). Classical historians and archaeologists confirm his accurate knowledge of Persian palaces, customs and manners. This includes the arrangement of the banquet (1:6-8), the seven nobles who formed the council of state (1:14), obeisance before the king and his favourites (3:2), belief in lucky and unlucky days (3:7), exclusion of mourning garb from the palace (4:2), hanging as the death penalty (5:14), the practice of dressing someone honoured by the king in the king's robes (6:8) and the dispatching of couriers with royal messages (3:13; 8:10).

The book's reception

The book has had a mixed reception — appreciated by some, and disliked by others. Later Jewish writers sought to explain away the opposition of their predecessors, and praised the book somewhat extravagantly. Rabbi Simeon b. Lakish (*c.* A.D. 300) ranked it next to the Law. Maimonides (A.D. 1134-1204), a great Jewish scholar and medieval rabbi, was so appreciative of it that he placed Esther second only in value to the Pentateuch and the Mosaic Law. He declared that although the Prophets and the Writings would pass away when Messiah came, the book of Esther and the Law would remain.

Martin Luther's reaction was the opposite: 'I was so hostile to this book [II Maccabees] and to Esther that I could wish they did not exist at all; for they Judaize too greatly and have much pagan impropriety.' He further complained that the book of Esther had a greater reputation among the Jews than Isaiah or Daniel. Martin Luther's outstanding contribution to the history of the church did not make him infallible! He also made a mistaken judgement about the New Testament letter of James, calling it 'a right strawy epistle'.

The historicity of Esther

Commentators who do not accept the inspiration of Scripture, and the providence of God in the remarkable formation of the canon of Scripture, often treat the book of Esther as legend rather than history, and as merely a book intended to explain the origin and significance of Purim. Significantly, they seldom offer reasons for their scepticism apart from the remarkable nature of the story of Esther itself. One feels like remarking, 'Remember the saying, "Truth is sometimes stranger than fiction."'

What must be said in defence of the historicity of the book of Esther is that it fits in perfectly with other Bible books, in the interval between the return of Zerubbabel to Jerusalem (537 B.C.) and that of Ezra (458 B.C.). Furthermore, the institution of Purim finds its only explanation in the Bible in this book, and that feast is still observed by Jews everywhere. Its references to 'the book of the annals' or 'the book of the chronicles' (2:23; 6:1; 10:2) firmly anchor it in history, as does its accurate presentation of life in the Persian court, as we know it from secular history. On a number of occasions we shall have cause to refer to secular historians whose comments coincide perfectly with the picture the book of Esther provides of Xerxes' times.

Its canonicity

The canon is the term given to the closed collection of the books of the Bible accepted as the inspired Scriptures. Esther's place in the canon was debated among both Jews and Christians. Its admission appears to have been initially delayed by the Jews, possibly because of the omission of God's name, the absence of vital aspects of the Jewish religion, the marriage of Esther to a non-Jew and its establishment of the Feast of Purim, a feast not laid down in the Mosaic Law.

Esther is the only Old Testament book not found among the Dead Sea Scrolls of the Essene community at Qumran, which dated from the second century B.C. to about the first century A.D. This may simply be an archaeological accident, in that it existed even though no fragment of it was found. Or it may mean that the Essene Community did not regard it as part of the Old Testament. However, it was recognized among the sacred books by Josephus, who identified Esther as the last book in its date of composition to have been admitted into the Jewish canon of Scripture.[11]

Esther finds its place in the Septuagint,[12] a Greek version of the Old Testament, said to have been made in the third century B.C. by seventy-two scholars in seventy-two days. There were at least two revisions of the Hebrew text of Esther, the longer of which was preserved in this Greek translation. It contains six extended passages, or supplements and, by including the name of God over fifty times, these make the book's religious tone more obvious and explicit. Jerome (*c.* 345 – *c.* 419), the translator of the Vulgate, the Latin version of the Bible, placed these additions to the Hebrew scroll at the very end of the story (after 10:3). They are included in the Apocrypha under the title, 'The Additions to the Book of Esther.' Ten verses are added to chapter 10, plus six more chapters. These contain a dream of Mordecai, in which he is supposed to have had a premonition of Haman's plot, and how it was to be defeated. It details Haman's decree, the prayer of Mordecai and Esther, the letters by which Xerxes revoked those procured by Haman, and the authorization of the feast of Purim. What is outstanding is the marked contrast between these chapters and the text of Esther in our Bible. They do not read as authentic, and they serve to confirm the authenticity of the book of Esther, as we possess it.

It seems that Esther was regarded as part of the Jewish canon by the time of the Council of Jamnia in A.D. 90, although debate continued both among Jews and Christians for a few centuries about its inclusion. It comes last in the five rolls that are read at the great festivals of the Jewish year (Song of Solomon, Ruth, Lamentations, Ecclesiastes and Esther), and is one of the most popular books among the Jews. It is called *the* Megillah (*the* Scroll) by Jewish readers on account of the enormous esteem in which it is held. It is inserted with the Law in the synagogue rolls and is treated with the highest reverence. There are more manuscripts of the book of Esther than of any other part of the Old Testament. More Jewish translations, interpretations and paraphrases (Targums) and homiletic commentaries (Midrashim) are based upon it than upon any other part. It is probably the case that more Jewish commentaries have been written upon it than upon any other book except the Law.

Although Esther is never quoted by our Lord Jesus Christ or any of the New Testament writers, there is evidence that early Christians regarded it as a book suitable for the beginner, no doubt because of its lively narrative and lessons about God's care of his people and the relationship of believers to a heathen state.

Some have suggested that the book was ignored in the early Christian centuries, but this is incorrect. Origen (*c.* 185 – *c.* 254) maintained the principle that all the Scriptures are accessible to every believer. He included Esther in the books that the youngest believers should read. Clement of Alexandria (*c.* 155 – *c.* 220) mentions the story of Esther, as do Eusebius (*c.* 265 – *c.* 339) and Augustine (354 – 430). Cyril of Jerusalem (*c.* 310 – 386) encouraged Christians to have nothing to do with apocryphal writings but to read the twenty-two books of the Old Testament, with the book of Esther as the twelfth of the historical books. In a festival letter in 367 Athanasius included Esther in a group of writings suitable for those receiving instruction in the Christian faith with a view to baptism.

In A.D. 397 the book of Esther was admitted to the Christian canon. It is probably right to suggest that it has been a neglected book. It is said that not a single Christian commentary was written on it during the first seven centuries. However, the clear inclusion of Esther in the thirty-nine books of the Old Testament is confirmed to have been a right decision the more we study and understand it, and appreciate the manner in which the Holy Spirit teaches important lessons by the events its narrative records.

(A list of books and articles published in the twentieth century lists some 700 titles of books and articles on Esther. Interest in the book reached its peak in the decade before the First World War, and was renewed in the 1950s after the Second, not surprisingly in view of the anti-Semitism that the intervening period sadly demonstrated.)

Christ in all the Scriptures

Since one of the most well-known facts about the book of Esther is the absence of God's name, it is plain, too, that there is no direct reference to the Messiah, our Lord Jesus Christ. The conversation our Saviour had with the two disciples on the Emmaus road on the day of his resurrection is revealing. 'He said to them, "How foolish you are, and how slow of heart to believe all that the prophets have spoken! Did not the Christ have to suffer these things and then enter his glory?" And beginning with Moses and all the Prophets, he explained to them what was said in all the Scriptures concerning himself.'[13] That encourages us to ask, 'Can we see Christ in the book of Esther?'

We do not know what use, if any, Jesus made of the book of Esther in that unique conversation on the Emmaus road. The word 'all' in Luke 24:27 does not have to mean that he went through every one of the thirty-nine books of the Old Testament. However, it does imply that he showed them everywhere in it that his coming was promised and anticipated, and that God's consistent purpose was the deliverance of his people, culminating in the greatest deliverance of all at the cross.

As Paul considered God's great saving purposes, he was compelled to exclaim:

> Oh, the depth of the riches of the wisdom and knowledge
>   of God!
>   How unsearchable his judgements,
>   and his paths beyond tracing out!
> 'Who has known the mind of the Lord?
>   Or who has been his counsellor?'
> 'Who has ever given to God,
>   that God should repay him?'
> For from him and through him and to him are all things.
>   To him be the glory for ever! Amen. [14]

The book of Esther shows how salvation is God's prerogative from first to last.

Three important truths are worthy of consideration. First, crucial to the background of the book of Esther is *the conflict described in God's words to the serpent, the devil's instrument,* in Genesis 3:15:

> And I will put enmity
>   between you and the woman,
>   and between your offspring and hers;
> he will crush your head,
>   and you will strike his heel.

Satan's activity is traceable throughout the Bible. His tracks may be discerned, together with the aliases he employs — in this case, that of Haman. Satan, the enemy of souls, was endeavouring to destroy the Jews, the people through whose seed the Messiah was to be born into the world, in order to make null and void God's promise of a Redeemer. The same enmity that inspired Haman also inspired Herod to give 'orders to kill all the boys in Bethlehem and its vicinity who were two years old and under, in accordance with the time he had learned from the Magi'.[15] As Jesus explained to the Samaritan woman, 'Salvation is from the Jews.'[16] God was committed to preserving the Jewish people so that from them salvation might go out into the ends of the earth, even though they failed him so often. It was because of this truth that the survival of the Jewish nation at the time of Esther was so important. God's protection of his people was the protection of the offspring of the woman[17] through which he preserved and carried on his plan of redemption. Satan was to strike 'the heel' of Esther and her people, but they were to crush his head in the complete defeat and overthrow of Haman and his wicked works. The book of Esther is a key chapter in redemption history.

Secondly, every time God raised up, entirely at his initiative, a deliverer of his people, *he anticipated and gave notice of the coming of the great and supreme Deliverer, his Son.* Many instances of deliverance in the history of the Jews were pictures and foreshadowings of Calvary. Individuals like Joseph, Moses, Gideon, Samson and David were all anticipations of David's 'greater Son'. So too was Esther. She was prepared to lay down her life for her people. In the event it was not required of her, as it was to be demanded of the Great Shepherd of the sheep. Nevertheless the willingness was there, and the truth that deliverance often requires sacrifice on the part of another. Significantly, when in 1492-93 Jews were expelled from Spain, this reawakened Jewish hopes for the advent of the Messiah and the final redemption that God promises. They saw their suffering as a necessary preliminary to the coming of the Messiah and their restoration as a people to

Palestine. The Jews' triumph over Haman, the seed of Amalek, was viewed as a foretaste of the final redemption when the seed of Amalek will be completely destroyed.

Thirdly, part of the glory of the Lord Jesus' coming into the world was *the grace that came with him*.[18] Behind God's control of unfavourable circumstances and his remarkable raising up of Esther to be her people's deliverer was God's grace, a grace to be perfectly made known and shown at the coming of his Son, Jesus Christ. It is perhaps noteworthy that Jewish tradition says that the Feast of Purim will be one tradition that will be preserved at the time of the Messiah.

1.
Majesty, alcohol and example

Please read Esther 1:1-22

When nothing seems to be happening spiritually, much may be taking place behind the scenes. If we had lived in the fifth century B.C., we might have come to the conclusion that God was doing little or nothing in the Persian Empire. We might have thought that perhaps he had forsaken his people, the Jews, many of whom were exiles scattered throughout its territories.

However, God was at work. Knowing the end from the beginning, as the God of knowledge, the Alpha and Omega,[1] he had already anticipated the problems that were to face the Jews, and his deliverance was on its way. That is an abiding principle of God's dealings with his people, now as then. What takes us by surprise does not catch him unawares!

The first chapter of Esther describes an incident in the court of the Persian Empire, providing the background for the dramatic events that were to follow. The narrative itself provides no obvious or outstanding clue as to the best way to interpret and apply it practically. However, it provides us with a clear illustration of 1 John 2:16-17, where John reminds us that the essence of worldliness is its lust for physical pleasures, its desires for everything we see and its pride in possessions, all of which will pass away.

Kingship means majesty

Ahasuerus (1:1, AV, NKJV), King of Persia, is commonly identified with Xerxes I (486–465 B.C.). The name **'Xerxes'** comes
from the Greek, which represents old Persian, meaning 'ruling over heroes' or 'he who rules over men'. 'Ahasuerus'
comes from the Hebrew rendering of the name. He was the
son of Darius I and Queen Atossa, the daughter of Cyrus, and
was in his thirties at his accession to the throne in November
486 B.C. He was less able than his father.[2]

Greek historians know Xerxes mostly as a commander of
armies on the battlefield. He and most of his brothers served
as generals and officers in the army. Herodotus draws attention to his handsome physical appearance, and in particular
his tallness: 'Of all those tens of thousands of men, for
goodliness and stature there was not one worthier than Xerxes
himself to hold that command.'[3] As soon as he succeeded his
father, he subdued a rebellion in Egypt. He then spent three
years preparing a huge fleet and army to punish the Greeks for
aiding the Ionian cities against Persia in 498 B.C. and for de-
feating the Persians at Marathon in 490 B.C. Herodotus estimated the combined strength of Xerxes' land and naval forces
as 2,641,610 men — an incredible total that has aroused considerable scepticism. No doubt, however, whatever the precise number, it was the largest mustering of forces ever known
up to that time.

The opening verses of the book describe six timeless trappings of kingship or authority.

1. Xerxes had dominion (1:1)

He **'ruled over 127 provinces ... from India'** — i.e. the
Indus valley — **'to Cush'** — i.e. Ethiopia, the modern Nubia,
or the upper Nile region. (The use of the past tense implies

that Xerxes was dead by the time Esther was written.) Under his father the Persian Empire was divided into twenty satrapies, each sub-divided for purposes of administration into a number of provinces. Xerxes' dominion extended from east to west — India and Ethiopia marked the two extreme boundaries of the then-known world.

In the royal palace at Persepolis, a palace of considerable magnificence, extravagance and lavishness, archaeologists discovered a foundation stone that confirms Xerxes' titles and his territorial claims mentioned in the book of Esther. It illustrates not only the extent of his territories, but his arrogance. It begins, 'I am Xerxes, the great king, the only king, the king of [all] countries [which speak] all kind of languages, the king of this [entire] big and far-reaching earth — the son of King Darius, the Achaemenian, a Persian, son of a Persian, an Aryan of Aryan descent.'[4] Herodotus confirms the extent of Xerxes' territories.[5] His empire was thought to be so vast that the sun never set upon it.

2. Xerxes had a royal throne (1:2)

Throughout the ages a throne has been a symbol of dominion and royal power. Xerxes' throne was in Susa, a city surrounded by mountains and streams. Persepolis was his capital in theory, and Susa, a citadel in Elam, 150 miles east of Babylon, located in modern Iran, not far from the Iraqi border, was his winter home. Susa was renowned for its fruit and flowers and, in particular, the lily that gave the city its name. Especially since the time of Darius, it had become more and more the magnificent and preferred official residence of the Persian kings.

Excavations at the site from 1852 onwards uncovered the hall and throne-room of the palace. The racial mixture of the Persian Empire is reflected in an inscription written in three languages on four columns. Further excavations from 1884 revealed that the ruined city had originally covered an area of almost five thousand acres. It was divided into four distinct districts: the citadel-mound, the palace, the city (the business and residential area) and the district on the plain to the west of the river. The palace itself had three courts of different sizes, surrounded by halls and apartments. Beautifully coloured glazed bricks decorated it. Various artefacts bearing Xerxes' name have been found in the excavations.

3. Xerxes gave banquets (1:3,5)

Banquets or feasts are a significant feature in the book of Esther. The term occurs twenty times in the book, and only twenty-four times elsewhere in the Bible. The narrative begins with two feasts given by Xerxes and ends with two instituted by Mordecai.

Greek writers describe in detail the fabulous feasts given by Persian rulers. They were lavish in scale, and not least in the number of guests invited. Such extravagances were deliberate attempts to draw attention to Xerxes' wealth and power. He invited all his nobles and officials, the military leaders of Persia and Media, and the governors of all his provinces. The banquet was held **'in the enclosed garden of the king's palace'** (1:5). The mention of the garden is significant because the Persians loved flowers, with the rose as their probable favourite. Both 'lilac' and 'tulip' are Persian names. 'Tulip' and 'turban' were originally the same word, and the big coloured turbans of the East resemble the shape of tulips.

The Greek translation of the Old Testament (the Septuagint) suggests that the banquet was arranged to celebrate the king's marriage. His **'third year'** would have been 483/2. It has been thought that the mention of the third year of the king's reign (1:3) implies that the intention of the banquet was to give Xerxes' guests confidence in his strength and resources to

defeat the Greeks, as it was about this time that, having conquered Egypt, he assembled at Susa the influential people of
his realm in order to make arrangements for the invasion of
Greece. Notice the reference to **'military leaders'** (1:3).

It appears to have been a Persian habit to hold consult-
ations about war and other important state affairs during meals.
We know from other sources that in the third year of his reign
Xerxes called together an assembly to consider an expedition
against Greece, and his banquet may have been combined with
this assembly.[6] 'After the conquest of Egypt, when he was on
the point of taking in hand the expedition against Athens,
Xerxes called a conference of the leading men in the country,
to find out their attitude towards the war and explain to them
his own wishes.'[7] As the book of Proverbs counsels, 'For wag-
ing war you need guidance, and for victory many advisers.'[8]
The Persian custom was not like ours, which is rather to do
important business first, and then to entertain. They did both
at the same time.

The king also arranged a second banquet **'for all the people
from the least to the greatest, who were in the citadel'**
(1:5). These would have been the ancillary staff involved in
the special assembly the king had convened, made up of a
variety of officials of varying importance — rather like the
entourage that accompanies government ministers when they
gather in international conferences.

The king's banquets were lavish in duration. Extravagance
and luxury were characteristic of eastern kings, and particularly the Persians. The first banquet lasted **'for a full 180 days'**
(1:4), roughly six months, and the second for **'seven days'**. A
six-month feast was in keeping with the general pattern of
things for Xerxes, in that it was a matter of royal principle that
everything he did had to be bigger and better than anything
that anyone had ever done before. It is likely that all the nobles
did not remain at court throughout the whole period of feasting

but took their turn, some leaving as others arrived. The banquets were almost certainly a deliberate public-relations exercise to boost morale in the empire with further military operations about to begin.

There is more than a suggestion of decadence in the duration of these banquets. The Bible does not condemn banquets, but indicates that there is a right and wrong time for them. To engage in feasting at an inappropriate moment, or in an unsuitable manner, is a sign that false standards are operating.[9]

4. Xerxes was capable of great displays of wealth (1:4,6)

He showed the riches of his royal glory and the splendour and pomp of his majesty (1:4). When his subjects arrived at the second party, or banquet, they saw white curtains and blue hangings caught up to silver rings by means of cords made of fine linen and purple (1:6). These, Xenophon tells us, were the royal colours of Persia. They saw **'marble pillars'** and **'couches of gold and silver on a mosaic pavement of porphyry, marble, mother-of pearl'** and precious stones (1:6). Porphyry is a beautiful and very hard rock, quarried in ancient times in Egypt, composed of red-and-white crystals. The exotic nature of the decor of the king's garden is expressed by the unusual and rare words used to describe it. The ornamentation of the palace had been transported from all over the known world. Drinks were served in a variety of goblets (1:7). Changes of drinking vessels at a royal entertainment were designed to display the abundance of the king's possessions. We can imagine the gasps of amazement, and the pointing of fingers in astonishment, as the guests witnessed the evidences of the king's wealth. The queen's ability to hold a banquet for the women at the same time similarly underlined the extent of the king's riches (1:9).

5. Xerxes could show considerable bounty (1:7)

Liberality marked all he bestowed on his guests. The royal wine was served in goblets of gold — everything was according to the status of the king. The royal wine was lavished upon his guests **'in keeping with the king's liberality'**. There was no thought or possibility of anything running out, or being in short supply.

6. Xerxes had great authority (1:8,10)[10]

He could give orders, and these had to be obeyed, even about the manner in which people should drink at the banquet (1:8). The Hebrew in verse 8 can be translated as 'Drinking was according to this rule' — the rule being stated in the next words: **'Each guest was allowed to drink in his own way.'** The usual pattern was probably that when the king drank, everyone else drank. On this occasion the king commanded that it should be otherwise: people should be free to drink as they chose. Everyone was to do as he wished. The word translated **'command'** in the NIV is 'law', a word used throughout the book of Esther in regard to all royal decisions, from simple instructions to stewards (as here), to the judicial sentence punishing an illegal action (4:11) and to royal edicts allowing genocide. The Persian Empire lived under a rule of law in every detail of life. Xerxes likewise had authority to command his queen to be brought before him (1:10-11). His banquets were opportunities for him to honour himself. He intended the display of Vashti's beauty to be the culminating moment of the feasts.

Kingship presupposes majesty — majesty displayed in dominion, a throne, banquets and displays of wealth, liberality and authority. The worldly symbols of kingship and authority have not altered significantly throughout the centuries.

Christians do not begrudge authorities these symbols because they know that proper authority and government are God's gift to humanity, and are ordained by him. All authorities that exist have been appointed by God.[11] Whoever resists authority opposes what God has appointed, and those who withstand it bring judgement upon themselves.[12] Those in authority, like all of us, must one day answer to God for the way in which they have exercised and fulfilled their responsibilities.

The King to whom all are subject

As the story of Esther proceeds, Xerxes is seen to be subject to the King, the Sovereign Lord, whose majesty surpasses all others. Xerxes proudly called himself 'the great king, the only king' in the inscription we quoted earlier. However, there is only one King of kings — our Lord Jesus Christ![13] Before his majesty all the frail trappings of human kingship pale.

1. Our Saviour and King, Jesus Christ, has dominion

He reigns not only from India to Ethiopia, but in and over every nation. He is not simply King of the earth, but King of the universe.[14] It was not without significance that 'Pilate had a notice prepared and fastened to the cross. It read: "JESUS OF NAZARETH, THE KING OF THE JEWS"' and was written in Aramaic, Latin and Greek.[15]

God the Father has raised our Lord Jesus Christ to the highest place, and has conferred upon him the name that is above all others.[16] There is no greater name! He rules over the living and the dead.[17] He is ruler over all who exercise rule in the world.[18] He is Lord over all lords, and King over all kings.[19] All powers and beings in the universe must ultimately bow the knee to him.[20]

2. Our Lord Jesus Christ has a throne

It is established in the heavens. In his vision on the isle of
Patmos John saw the Lamb standing in the middle of the
throne.[21] It was a vision of the Lord Jesus on his throne that
Isaiah saw in the temple.[22]

3. Our Saviour has his own special banquets

The first, to which he invites his subjects, whenever they are
able to come, is what we know as the Lord's Supper. There is
no banquet on earth to compare with this. It is a love feast for
pardoned sinners, whatever their status in human society. The
bread and wine are the symbols of his broken body and his
outpoured blood, all for the sake of our salvation. This banquet is a foretaste of a far greater banquet to come — the
marriage feast of the Lamb. Then we shall sit down and feast
with him.[23]

4. Our heavenly King possesses immeasurable wealth

Well may we speak of his 'unsearchable riches'![24] The truly
rich one, he is rich in glory[25] and grace.[26] He is the source of
unimaginable liberality and generosity. The life he gives is eternal life. The glory to which he calls us is eternal glory. The
grace he bestows is boundless.

5. Our Saviour and King Jesus Christ has final authority

All authority in heaven and on earth has been given to him by
the Father.[27] As the exalted Lord, he is worthy to receive sovereign power.[28]

Those Jews to whom we have yet to be introduced in this
book were given discernment to see that beyond Xerxes, with
all his human majesty, there was a King of greater authority.

Without Xerxes' ever being aware of it, it was this King who
had deigned to give him the authority he possessed. That assurance influenced the Jews' prayers, hopes and actions. So too
should our Lord and Saviour's kingship inspire us to pray, to
hope and to act. Our prayers are stimulated and encouraged
as we remember we are coming to our King.

All King Xerxes' majesty, wealth and prestige disappeared
and, likewise, all who put their confidence in him. How different, however, is the majesty, wealth and prestige of Jesus Christ,
the King of kings, our Saviour, and those throughout the centuries who have put their trust in him! Because he lives, they
live.[29] Because he reigns in glory, so too do they.[30]

Alcohol and the danger of mistakes

King Xerxes was **'in high spirits from wine'** — literally, 'the
heart was good' (1:10). The implication is that he was to some
degree intoxicated.[31] Since Jews considered the heart to be the
centre of thought, verse 10 could be translated, 'On the seventh day, when wine had gone to the king's head...' No doubt
on impulse, he gave the order for Queen Vashti to be brought
before his assembled guests (1:10-11). (Herodotus indicates
that Xerxes' queen was Amestris, rather than Vashti.[32] However, by assuming certain phonetic modifications, it has been
shown that Vashti can be identified with Amestris.[33] Herodotus
describes Amestris as a rather unpleasant character.[34] She is
presented as ruthless, powerful and influential, once taking
horrible revenge on a woman with whom her husband had
been in love.)

Xerxes' seven chamberlains, who were eunuchs,[35] were instructed to bring Vashti, wearing her royal crown (1:10-11).
The king wanted to display before both the ordinary people
and his princes her extraordinary beauty (1:11). A repeated

emphasis upon beauty occurs in the book.[36] However, he would not have wanted to put her beauty on show in such a public manner had his judgement not been influenced by the wine he had drunk. Alcohol can hamper our better judgement. It may rob us of our brains.

Queen Vashti declined! She probably did so because of the lewdness that her unexpected appearance at such a gathering would have occasioned. Strangers were not allowed to look at the beauty of Persian wives,[37] and Queen Vashti's defiance, therefore, was a modest and totally justifiable refusal to appear before a group of men who, if not drunk, were probably on the verge of intoxication.

Queen Vashti may have been a woman before her time. Her refusal, however, enraged the king, and his anger burned within him (1:12). His anger needs to be seen in the light of the honour-based society of which the king was head. To shame the king by disobedience was bound to produce the most extreme response. The greater the emphasis we place upon human status, the angrier we become when it is placed in jeopardy. Xerxes' anger clearly had a habit of arising and then subsiding.[38] When kings were all-powerful, all feared their anger.[39] Furious, Xerxes set in motion irrevocable disciplinary action against her. The counsel of the book of Proverbs is relevant: 'A fool shows his annoyance at once, but a prudent man overlooks an insult.'[40]

Two key questions need to be asked. First, would Xerxes have commanded Vashti to be brought before his guests — rather like a piece of furniture — if he had been completely sober? Secondly, if he had been sober, would he have become so angry?[41]

This is one of the most telling illustrations in the Bible of the danger of alcohol. The Christian attitude to drink is often a matter of debate. The arguments sometimes obscure the perfect balance the Bible strikes. Wine — the principal drink mentioned in the Bible — is among God's good gifts.[42] It is

regarded as a natural part of food and drink[43] and was offered
to God as a drink offering with some of the Old Testament
sacrifices[44] and also as part of the first-fruits of harvest.[45] It
may add to the pleasures of daily living, gladdening the heart,[46]
although it is folly to see it as a means of achieving happiness
and contentment.[47] The apostle Paul recognized its medicinal
value.[48]

When taken to excess anything good becomes unhelpful,
and sometimes positively bad. The Bible gives many warnings
about the danger of excessive drinking. Lingered over, and
drunk in excess, it can lead us astray,[49] as it befuddles the mind,[50]
making us indifferent to other people's feelings, insensitive to
propriety and prone to rash action, as in this record of Xerxes'
behaviour. It is said that Joseph Stalin, the Soviet Communist
leader, seldom drank himself, but deliberately lavished alcohol
on his colleagues and officials in order to loosen their tongues,
and to discover weaknesses he could exploit. Moderation in
everything, and not least in drinking, is imperative.[51]

The New Testament lifts the debate to a higher level by
explaining the importance of example, and our proper concern for the influence of our conduct upon our fellow believers.[52] Christian conduct at its best is not governed simply by
what is permissible, but what is beneficial.[53] Part of self-control
— an aspect of the Spirit's fruit in us — may be abstinence,
not because of 'black-and-white' convictions about drink, but
for the sake of dedication to God,[54] as in the case of the Old
Testament Nazirites (although sometimes this was only for a
limited period)[55] and John the Baptist.[56]

The New Testament draws a contrast between being filled
with wine and being filled with the Spirit.[57] Filled with the Spirit,
we become sensitive to other people's feelings. Filled with the
Spirit, we see the wisdom of proper proprieties and we observe
them. Filled with the Spirit, we feel his restraint when we are
tempted to take rash action.

Christians know the Lord Jesus to be both their Saviour and King. As Saviour, he delivers us from sins that would spoil and mar our lives. As King, he rules in our hearts. As his subjects, we want the control of our lives to be his alone. We are duty bound, therefore, not to hand over the direction of our lives to anything that threatens his rightful control. Above all, we desire to please him.[58]

Our relationship to God through our Lord Jesus Christ brings a new discipline to our life, impossible of achievement by any other means. In his Reith Lectures, John Galbraith describes how Karl Marx's last years were not a happy time for him. 'His health was bad and not improved by the abuse to which he had long subjected himself in matters of food, sleep, tobacco and alcohol.' One of the most influential thinkers and writers of the modern world was unable to control his appetites.

When the Lord Jesus rules our lives, he delivers us from habits that abuse our bodies and freedom, as well as mistakes to which those habits and unhelpful influences might lead us.

Example means influence

Upon Queen Vashti's refusal to come before his assembled guests to display her exceptional beauty, King Xerxes sought advice. The group of seven wise men were an established institution in the Persian court (1:13-14). They were supposed to be gifted in astrology, and knowledgeable about the laws and customs of the Persian Empire. The description in verse 13 is interesting: **'He spoke with the wise men who understood the times.'** This is similar to the expression used in 1 Chronicles 12:32 with regard to the members of the tribe of Issachar, although in a very different context. Ordinarily, the Persian king was physically inaccessible, but these advisers were so trusted and intimately associated with him that they

'had special access to the king' — literally, they 'saw the face of the king' (1:14).

What evidence we have from secular historians indicates that Xerxes was all too easily swayed between opposing counsels, not always having a clear mind of his own. He asked the question: **'According to law, what must be done to Queen Vashti? ... She has not obeyed the command of King Xerxes that the eunuchs have taken to her'** (1:15).

It is part of the wisdom of kings to take counsel from trusted advisers.[59] However, all counsel that advisers may give is subject to God's sovereignty and the outworking of his purposes. As Job affirmed, 'He silences the lips of trusted advisers and takes away the discernment of elders.'[60] The conclusion of the king's experts in matters of law and justice was plain: the queen had done wrong, not only against the king but also against all his subjects (1:16). It was recognized that the wives of those in positions of authority may have a profound influence on the conduct of other women (1:17-18). Everything that happened to the King of Persia was significant to the Persian people — nothing could be regarded as unimportant. What Queen Vashti had dared to do would become known everywhere. The king's advisers were concerned lest her action should prove a hindrance to men ruling over their households (1:17-18,22). They feared the rise of feminism in the Persian Empire.

In recent decades those dissatisfied with feminine role models both in Judaism and Christianity have seized upon the book of Esther as an area of special study for their cause and its inspiration. Those promoting African women's struggle for liberation in South Africa have used it in a similar way. Women's rights and liberation are important issues but they are not what the book of Esther is about, and its use in this way obscures the truths it is intended to convey.

The outcome was that Queen Vashti was to be queen no longer. She was never again to come before the king (1:19).

The counsel of Memucan, the spokesman for the advisers, was followed. Kings and rulers were very much in the hands of those who advised them. The advisers tended to be flatterers, prone to advise what they knew would please their master, since their livelihood and position depended on their pleasing him. How different is the Christian's Counsellor — the Holy Spirit[61] — who always tells us the truth and wants the best for us!

The practice of issuing a royal decree, or writing an additional one, to suit a particular situation seems to have been usual.[62] Vashti's position, as queen, was to be given to another (1:19). At the same time a decree was issued with the purpose of underlining the principle of the proper submission of wives to their husbands (1:20). It almost goes without saying that this was not the best way to achieve their purpose. In the treatment of his wife, the king had already set a bad example of trying to force respect, rather than behaving towards her in a way that won it. As is sadly often the case with monarchs, rulers and governments, Xerxes tried to impose on others what he had been unable to achieve himself. No indication is given of any recognition on the king's part of either sorrow or repentance at his action. His temper had got the better of his judgement. Passion had blinded reason. If he and his counsellors considered Vashti's example damaging, theirs was worse.

Xerxes used the fast courier service that Darius had established throughout the empire. This great Persian system of communications, a pony express, was considered the fastest means of human communication.[63] It would later be used to spread the document containing the incitement to murder (3:13), the countermeasure to it (8:9-14) and, presumably, the letters establishing the festival of Purim (9:20,29).

While it is impossible to justify Xerxes' harsh rejection of Vashti, his advisers were correct in appreciating the tremendous influence her act of disobedience would have upon other wives throughout the realm (1:17). They would refer to her bold and courageous example, and might, as a consequence, be prompted to repudiate the authority of their own husbands if their requests were similarly unreasonable. In this way family peace would have been threatened in fifth-century Persia — or so the king and his counsellors thought.

The subject of influence is an important issue, and one frequently raised in the Bible. We all exercise our greatest influence by example, whether good or bad, and provide role models of something to someone. A husband's example influences his wife, and vice versa. Have we not observed how married couples grow to be like one another? Parents' example influences their children's character and behaviour, with children not only looking like their parents but behaving like them.

Similarly, the example of spiritual leaders in a local church has a lot to do with the atmosphere that pervades its corporate life. The more prominent we are, or the more in the public eye, the greater tends to be our influence and responsibility for others.

We become helpful examples as we conscientiously fulfil our proper duties. The example husbands set influences, in turn, their sons when they become husbands. In the same way, the example wives set influences their daughters when the time comes for them to get married. And so we could go on.

All Christians should be examples of what is good because of uncompromising commitment to the example of the Lord Jesus — the Supreme Example. As we follow him as we ought, we become a helpful example to others so that, ideally, we are able to say, 'Whatever you have learned or received or heard from me, or seen in me — put it into practice.'[64]

Whenever we fail to be examples, we should take ourselves to task. If we have responsibility as spiritual leaders for disciplining others, we should take gracious, yet firm action when a bad example may grievously harm others, causing them to stumble.

The best counsel, both from the point of view of achieving self-control and that of setting a good example, as we established earlier, is to be filled with the Spirit, whose fruit is self-control.[65]

The first chapter of Esther is an encouragement to rejoice in the majesty and glory of our Lord Jesus Christ, especially as we compare his everlasting majesty with the passing glory of all kings, queens, presidents, dictators and public figures. We should keep our eyes fixed upon him, the Lord of glory.[66]

We should beware of anything that might remove our lives from the gracious control of God's Spirit, whether it is alcohol, love of possessions, or preoccupation with the cares of this life and the lure of wealth.

We should endeavour to be examples of godliness, of genuine Christlikeness, so that we glorify God by our daily life and build up and help all with whom we are in any way associated. None of us lives without influencing others, either for good or evil.

As we move from the first chapter to the second, the scene has been set for what is to follow and shows what Esther will be up against as she lives in the royal court.

2.
God is working
his purposes out!

Please read Esther 2

'**Later when the anger of King Xerxes had subsided, he remembered Vashti and what she had done and what he had decreed about her**' (2:1). Xerxes' anger was to flare up and then subside like this again on a later occasion (7:7,10).

He 'remembered', or he 'thought back'. The Authorized (or King James) Version's 'He remembered Vashti ... and *what was decreed* against her' (emphasis added) is a better translation than 'what *he* had decreed about her'. The passive verb indicates that what had been decreed had not been his independent decision. It may also suggest that he was transferring the blame for the decision onto his advisers, a tendency among rulers. A Midrash (a Jewish homiletic commentary) relates that when Xerxes was told what had happened to Vashti, he was infuriated with his advisers and banished them.[1] (The book of Esther does not tell us what happened to her.) Another version says that he had his advisers beheaded. Neither of these suggestions may be true, but they may indicate that Xerxes did not regard the decision about Vashti as wholly his own. The picture of Xerxes as an erratic, tyrannical and emotional man agrees with the estimate of him made by secular historians.[2]

It would appear that the years of the disastrous Greek war — with the campaign of Thermopylae and the battle of Salamis

— intervene between chapters 1 and 2. Xerxes' attack on Greece is one of the most famous military expeditions in world history. He is famous, or infamous, as the Persian king who led the unsuccessful invasion of Greece in 480 B.C., rendered memorable ever afterwards by the narrative of Herodotus in books 7 to 9 of his history. 'The army was indeed greater than any other in recorded history. There was not a nation in Asia that he did not take with him against Greece; save for the great rivers there was not a stream his army drank from that was not drunk dry. Some nations provided ships, others formed infantry units; from some cavalry was requisitioned, from others horse-transports and crews; from others, again, warships for floating bridges, or provisions and naval craft of various kinds.'[3]

Xerxes demanded submission from all the Greek states, but most refused. As a consequence, he decided to lead a carefully prepared expedition of about 180,000 men into Greece through Thrace and Macedonia. Beginning with victories, he ended with defeats. When this chapter opens four years have passed, years in which he has not had time to choose a new queen. The years between the deposition of Vashti and the coronation of Esther (cf. 2:16) may be identified with this period during which Xerxes was absent on his expedition against Greece.

A gloriously reassuring theme of the book of Esther is that God is in control. He is in command of human actions and human delays. The background to his purposes is his sovereignty and providence. God's sovereignty is his supreme authority and absolute dominion: he rules over everything, and does what he will.[4] In this book Israel defeats her enemies without having a human king, underlining the lesson of Psalm 75:6-7:

No one from the east or the west
   or from the desert can exalt a man.

But it is God who judges:
he brings one down, he exalts another.

God's providence is his good, kind and unceasing activity
and control of all things so that everything happens as he decided long ago, and for the good of his people.[5] He watches
over the interests of each of his children as if he had no other
creature for whom to care. Nothing escapes his notice, or happens without his permission. Even the worst things will work
out for our good. We see only links in the chain, but God sees
the end from the beginning, as the source, guide and goal of
all that is.[6] His providence is not limited to one age or period
of time for, as Psalm 90:1 declares, 'Lord, you have been our
dwelling-place throughout all generations.' Sovereignty and
providence are attributes of our King.[7] This chapter reveals
that when things seem to be a matter of luck, God is achieving
his goals. Providence, not chance, rules.[8]

The mystery of God's providence

There is a mystery — so far as we are concerned — about
God's providence. He is the Creator and we are his creatures.
He is infinite, and we are finite. There are features of his dealings with us which he chooses to reveal. However, there are
other aspects that he determines to keep hidden until that time
when we are to know everything completely, just as he knows
us now.[9]

It is usually quite presumptuous for us to suggest how God
will choose to exercise his sovereignty. We know that he will
always do so in complete and utter consistency with his holiness and love. But in terms of his government of the nations,
and his future direction of our lives, we cannot foresee the

detailed outworking of his dominion. Nevertheless we can look back on the events of history, and of our own lives, and discern how God has worked everything together for good.[10]

God never fails to anticipate his people's needs, whether personal or corporate. The whole of the Old Testament demonstrates this reassuring truth, whether in his sending of Joseph ahead to Egypt, so that he might become the saviour of his people, or in the preservation of Moses so that he likewise might become their God-appointed leader into freedom. Joseph in Egypt was able to declare to his brothers, 'So then, it was not you who sent me here, but God.'[11]

The circumstances of this chapter are not dissimilar. A key person is soon going to be necessary and indispensable for the preservation of the Jews (chapter 3). To achieve this important providence in their history, God used first the displacing of a heathen queen. The request the king made of the queen was his own (1:10-11), and so too was Vashti's refusal (1:12). God, however, used the consequences to bring about good for his chosen people.

God's controlling activity behind the scenes

We may recognize a number of factors — six in all — in which God's control of the situation may be discerned.

1. The suggestion of the king's advisers (2:2-4)

After the exhausting rigours of war in his ill-fated expedition to Greece, the king felt the lack of Vashti's companionship, and needed someone to take her place.

He was probably extremely miserable upon his return. Herodotus narrates that in the midst of his glory on his march to Greece, Xerxes said, 'In this short life there is no man either among these or others so happy, that he should not often and more than once be in such a position as to prefer death to life. The misfortunes come, and diseases rage, which make our life appear so long, though it is so short.' It is significant that he said this in spite of all his displays of wealth.

It would appear to have been the initiative of the king's attendants to suggest that beautiful young virgins should be sought out for the king, from among whom he could make his choice (2:2). They were most specific in their recommendations. Commissioners in all the provinces of his kingdom were to be appointed to bring these young women into the women's quarters in Susa, the capital (2:3).

'Harem' (2:3) is an Arabic word meaning, literally, 'that which is prohibited or unlawful', that is to say, a sacred place, and was first used in the seventeenth century. It is not an unreasonable translation, but the literal translation 'house of women' is preferable. Virginity and beauty were the two criteria. In many ways it bore the character of a national beauty contest, although a much more serious affair.

These young women were to be committed to the care of Hegai, the king's eunuch in charge of the women. All the necessary cosmetics of the day were to be provided for them (2:3). Then in due course the one who was most acceptable to the king was to become queen in the place of the deposed Vashti. The whole idea pleased the king, and he acted upon it (2:4). The king's pleasure finds particular emphasis.[12]

Neither Esther nor Mordecai could have suggested or put into the mind of the king or his advisers this way of choosing a new queen — a procedure that was to bring Esther to the fore. But God could do so, and he did! It would have been more natural and usual for the king to take a wife from one of the seven noble families of Persia. The Persian king was

supposedly obliged to choose his wife from one of those families.[13] However, a rule of this kind could easily be broken.
Darius, Xerxes' father, had married outside of these families.

The hearts of rulers are in God's control. God could speak
of Cyrus II (539–530 B.C.), a Persian ruler, as 'his anointed ...
whose right hand I take hold of'.[14] 'The king's heart is in the
hand of the Lord; he directs it like a watercourse wherever he
pleases.'[15] The king's advisers were, without their knowledge,
under God's direction. The initiative advisers to heads of governments take may often be a reflection of the prior initiative
of God's Spirit. While often we may feel ourselves to be at the
mercy of the unpredictable wills of others, we are, in fact, in
God's hands. All who appear to have control of us are under
his control.

2. Esther's natural beauty and background (2:7)

The king was not choosing a queen on the grounds of noble
birth or aristocratic background, but of beauty. Esther had
neither the first nor the second, but she did possess natural
beauty and charm. Josephus maintained that she 'surpassed all
women in beauty' in the entire habitable world.[16] Later rabbis
maintained that she was one of the four most beautiful women
in history, along with Sarah, Rahab and Abigail.[17] It was an
unwise way to choose a wife since outward attractiveness may
cover inner ugliness. A young Methodist minister, later well
known as Dr William Sangster of Westminster, startled the
Welsh town in which he served by holding a beauty competition.
The condition of entry was different from what was usual, in
that all contestants had to be over seventy. His argument was
that at seventeen you have the face that God gave you, but
that at seventy you have the face you have made for yourself.
'Charm is deceptive, and beauty is fleeting; but a woman who

fears the LORD is to be praised.'[18] Fortunately for Xerxes, Esther both feared the Lord and had beauty.

Esther's Hebrew name was **'Hadassah'** (2:7). **'Esther'** picks up the sound of the Hebrew and suggests the star-like flowers of the myrtle. In the prophets the myrtle was to replace the briars and the thorns, thus depicting God's forgiveness and acceptance of his people.[19] Jews in Babylon seem often to have received foreign names.[20] Like Daniel, Esther had two names, one Hebrew and the other not, the latter being derived either from the Persian *strara*, or star, or from Ishtar, the Babylonian goddess of love. It may have been conferred on her because of her outstanding beauty. On the other hand, it may have been a name she used initially to draw attention away from her Jewish identity. Hadassah indicated her Jewish origins, something Mordecai wished her to conceal at this stage.

Esther had neither father nor mother alive, and had been brought up by her cousin Mordecai (2:7). Much older than Esther, he adopted her as his daughter upon her parents' death. **'Mordecai'** is a Babylonian name that incorporates the name of the Babylonian state god. It may be a Hebrew version of the common name Mardukaya.

Mordecai was the son of Jair, son of Shimei, son of Kish (2:5), and may have been related to the clan of Saul.[21] His family had been carried into exile from Jerusalem among those whom Nebuchadnezzar, King of Babylon, had carried away with Jehoiachin, King of Judah (2:5-6). The captivity took place in 597 B.C. and Xerxes began to reign in 485 B.C. — 112 years later. A careful reading of the Hebrew text shows that it is grammatically possible to infer that verses 5 and 6 are not saying that Mordecai himself was taken captive in 597, for that would have made him 120 years old. The relative pronoun 'who' in verse 6 refers not to Mordecai, but to his great-grandfather Kish.

Esther possessed natural beauty and charm (2:7). The Hebrew says literally that she was **'beautiful in form and lovely to look at'**. That was all part of God's gracious providence. We have no choice over the natural beauty or attractiveness with which we are born. We have little choice over the personalities we develop either. But God our Creator has the power to make us what he wants us to be. Before our conception he knew everything about us, and he can determine the characteristic features of our lives. As David put it, 'You created my inmost being; you knit me together in my mother's womb.'[22]

Esther might have been born a girl of merely ordinary beauty, or even ugly. But, in God's control of things for his sovereign purposes, she was not. She might have been born into a situation where there was no kind relative to care for her when she was orphaned, but in God's providence she was well looked after.

God knows best what is good and necessary for his children. So often our frustrations arise from our wishing the circumstances of either the past or the present were different. 'If only I had not been an only child!' says one, while another says, 'If only I had not had brothers and sisters!' Or, perhaps comparing ourselves with others, we say, 'If only I had been better looking!' Our highest wisdom is to submit to all the circumstances of life as they are, and not to dwell on what we would wish them to be, but rather to recognize God's gracious control over them and rest in his perfect knowledge and concern for us.

3. Esther's selection for the group out of which the new queen was to be chosen (2:3,8).

The king's order and edict were duly published. The mention of **'the king's order and edict'** and our knowledge of the unrepealable nature of the laws of the Persians (e.g., 1:19) point to the inescapable nature of Esther's compliance. Many girls were brought to Susa to be committed to the care of Hegai. According to Josephus, there is evidence that 400 girls were brought, showing that the competition between them must have been considerable. There was far more to be gained than from any contemporary 'Miss World' contests! Imagine ambitious mothers and grandmothers grooming their daughters or granddaughters for the selection committee of their province! Esther had neither mother nor grandmother to guide her. But the one true God was her God. Her beauty was his gift, as was her charm. We are not at all surprised that she was chosen to be among the pool from which the new queen was to be selected. At this stage, however, Esther cannot have had any idea of what was going to happen.

God's will was being worked out. His will is always good, pleasing and perfect.[23] Our privilege as Christians is to accept and rejoice in it, even before it has been made plain. Our Saviour set an example of delighting in the Father's will.[24] In his Father's will was his peace.

When God's will is our delight and pleasure we may rest at all times in the certainty that it will be done in our lives as certainly as it is in heaven. On occasions it may appear as if the direction of our lives is in the hands of others — rather like the selection committees in the Persian provinces — but the outcome is always with God. This assurance frees us from fretfulness, as well as the snare of selfish competitiveness. If we are wise, whatever God reckons as right for us, we want — nothing more and nothing less.

The full period of the preparation prescribed for the women was twelve months — **'six months with oil of myrrh and six with perfumes and cosmetics'** (2:12). It has been suggested that one of the reasons for this long period of time was to ensure that the young women were chaste, and therefore not pregnant, so that the king might not be imposed upon, or obliged to be regarded as the father of a child that was in fact not his. But there seems to be no evidence for the justice of this suggestion.

The phrase **'perfumes and cosmetics'** (2:12) means literally 'fumigation with other cosmetics'. Persia and India, together with Arabia, were renowned for aromatic perfumes. We know that cosmetic incense burners were used in the ancient world. These periods of beauty treatment involved the extensive use of fumigation, with both hygienic and therapeutic purposes in view. Various pastes applied to the skin over an extended period could lighten its colour and remove spots and blemishes. Attention to outward physical beauty is a long-drawn-out process!

Twelve months' beauty treatment of the most intensive kind was embarked upon in each girl's case. Verse 9 indicates that nutrition was not neglected, for as well as the supply of cosmetics, **'special food'** was provided. When the time came for a girl to go to the king, **'Anything she wanted was given to her to take with her from the harem to the king's palace'** (2:13). Presumably she could choose her own clothes, accessories and perfumes.

While we can understand Xerxes' natural human attraction to physical beauty, we have to recognize how foolish he was. Far more desirable is inner loveliness, 'the unfading beauty of a gentle and quiet spirit'.[25] Such a spirit is a manifestation of holiness. It is clear from this narrative as it progresses that Esther's inner beauty more than matched her good looks. She was not only physically beautiful but also appealing in personality; she was not only good to look at but a delight to know. Her mind and character were as pleasing as her physical appearance. These advantages were all part of God's gift to Esther that made her choice by others inevitable.

4. The favour Esther gained with those in whose custody she was placed (2:8-9)

Many young women were taken into the king's palace for the intensive course of beauty treatment, and put into Hegai's care. We are told that Esther pleased Hegai, and **'won his favour'** (2:9). She 'took' or 'gained' his favour, or kindness. This idiom is unique in the Old Testament to the book of Esther and suggests that her social skills gained her favour. Again we discern that she was more than a pretty face.

Remembering that, for reasons of his own, the writer of the book of Esther does not mention God's name, we may interpret this favour in the same way as the writer of Genesis does regarding the favour Joseph gained in Egypt: 'While Joseph was there in the prison, the LORD was with him; he showed him kindness and granted him favour in the eyes of the prison warder.'[26] Daniel's experience was the same. God caused an 'official to show favour and sympathy to Daniel'.[27] The favour Esther knew was a similar gift from God. Why should Hegai have taken such a special interest in Esther above the others? The explanation that makes sense is that God disposed his heart in this way. Hegai quickly provided Esther with her ointments, her portion of food and seven chosen maids from the king's palace. He advanced her and her maids to **'the best place'** in the house of women (2:9).

Favour is never something a Christian should court. To do so may often involve compromise. Compromising Christian standards, whatever the apparently good ends in view, is never the Christian way. However, when we are in God's will and aim to do it, we may count upon him to provide us with sufficient favour with others — individuals or authorities — to ensure that we are able to fulfil his purposes. Esther proved it to be so, and so have faithful believers throughout the centuries.

The book that comes before Esther in the Old Testament, Nehemiah, records how Nehemiah gained favour in the eyes of the king so that he likewise was able to do God's will.[28] As we properly seek God's favour, we may depend upon him to give us whatever human goodwill and help we may need to do the same.

5. The good advice Esther received (2:10,15)

Mordecai gave her instruction. He acted as a father to her. He forbade her to reveal her nationality and family background (2:10). We are not told why he instructed her in this way. The Septuagint describes Mordecai as having a dream foretelling the crisis and how it would be met. While this cannot be proved, it would seem to indicate that wisdom was given to him to anticipate the problems of his people, for which he took appropriate precautions, sensing that there was some special purpose behind Esther's surprising status in the king's court.

Good advice came also from *Hegai* (2:15). Some in Persia were 'in the know' when it came to understanding what the king would be looking for in a potential queen. Hegai, the king's eunuch, proffered advice to Esther. So far as we know, there was no reason for him to do so, but he did. Esther was careful to follow his directions. When the time came for her to make the acquaintance of the king, she asked for nothing except what Hegai advised. This response was due in part at least to the good training she had received from Mordecai, for she knew the place and priority of obedience, as God's Word teaches.[29]

The advice Esther received — and we do not know its precise details — plainly proved to be the best, and God's gift to her. Part of his gracious providence in our lives is the provision of people who give us wise counsel. Sometimes God may graciously bring someone across our path who has the information, the guidance and the exact help we require. To the world at large it may seem an accident, but we know it to be otherwise.

6. The immediate and overwhelming attraction the king felt for Esther so that he chose her as his queen (2:17)

The momentous day came for Esther to be brought before him. The month of Tebeth (the tenth month of the Jewish calendar, corresponding to our December-January) of his seventh year would have been either December 479 or early January 478. The words, **'she was taken'** (2:16) imply Esther's passivity, or necessary compliance, in all that took place. We can imagine her nervousness. Maybe she had some inkling that the recent surprising events pointed to an exciting outcome.

It would seem to have been a case of love at first sight. The king more than liked Esther; he fell in love with her. The Hebrew word for 'love' implies a significant emotional bond. He loved Esther more than all the women; she found grace and favour in his sight more than all the other virgins.

The choice was clear, and the decision was made. King Xerxes set the royal crown upon her head and made her queen instead of Vashti (2:17). **'The king gave a great banquet, Esther's banquet, for all his nobles and officials. He proclaimed a holiday throughout the provinces and distributed gifts with royal liberality'** (2:18). Everyone had a holiday, and was encouraged to share the king's joy. The author of the book of Esther may want us to appreciate that when things go well with the Jews, other people benefit.

The assembling of the virgins **'a second time'** has prompted considerable discussion, for we cannot be dogmatic about its purpose. Literally, verse 19 reads: 'when virgins were gathered again'. The author does not explain why. One suggestion is that, in the context of Esther's coronation, there was a second procession of the unsuccessful candidates, all of whom were beautiful and charming, to set off in even more striking relief Esther's beauty. These were then sent back home at the conclusion of the coronation ceremonies. Another suggestion is that it has to do with the point at which these other young women were moved to the second harem, under a different keeper, having become concubines. Verse 19 is not expanded upon because the focus of the story is upon the choice of Esther.

God's control of events to bring about his purposes

To whose hand are we to trace this important selection of Esther as queen, a choice that was to have such great significance later? Without doubt, we must trace it to the hand of God. None of these events was within her power. She could not have suggested how the king should go about finding a new queen. She had had nothing to do with the development of her natural beauty. She could not have ensured that she was chosen as a candidate for queenship. She could not have been sure of gaining favour with Hegai, the king's representative. She could not have expected preferential treatment. She certainly could not have made the king choose her. But God could influence, control and direct all of these things, and he did! However, none of those concerned — with perhaps the exception of Mordecai and Esther — recognized the unseen hand of God in what was happening.

During the time of these proceedings **'Mordecai was sitting at the king's gate'** (2:19,21). Sitting at the king's gate may imply that Mordecai held some government office or status rather than simply stating where he was to be found day by day. The phrase implies a position of privilege or responsibility. (Mordecai is an example of saints in 'Caesar's household', as found in the New Testament.[30]) Persian officials had to stay at the gate of the royal palace.[31] Throughout the ancient Near East 'the gate' was the area where trials were conducted and justice dispensed.[32] This function continued after the exile period. While those making a formal complaint stood during the proceedings, the judge, who might be the king, or his appointee, 'sat'.[33]

It has been suggested that after Esther had been made queen, she was instrumental in bringing about Mordecai's appointment as a judge. Not only was this recognition of what Mordecai had done for her, but also it made communication with him easier.

The concluding verses of chapter 2 record Mordecai's commendable action in making known to the authorities, through Esther, a conspiracy hatched against the king (2:21-23). **'Found out'** (2:22) implies that he had access to secret and confidential information, but no indication is given as to how he obtained it. For the present this public-spirited action went unrewarded. If we had been alive at the time, and aware of the facts, we might have drawn a contrast between the unrewarded merit of Mordecai and the unmerited prizes given to Haman, in which he revelled.

No comment is made concerning Mordecai's public-spirited act. Its importance must not be overlooked, because of what was going to happen later in chapter 6. God's providence is at work in seemingly small things, the importance of which we may not recognize at the time. In spite of all that might have appeared to the contrary, God was overruling everything. And that is always the case! Such an evidence of God's control does not stand alone in the Bible.

The greatest demonstration of God's sovereignty was the cross of our Lord Jesus Christ. To the human eye the crucifixion appeared total failure and disaster. Human sin and wickedness were seen at their worst. But God was in control. Behind the scenes he was working out his eternal purposes. Our Saviour's death and all its circumstances were according to God's prearranged plan for the achievement of our salvation. When our Lord appeared to be in human hands alone, his eyes were upon his Father. To quote one of the Messianic psalms:

> I have set the LORD always before me.
> > Because he is at my right hand,
> > I shall not be shaken.[34]

God was working out his purposes.

God is indeed working out his purposes! This assurance has practical repercussions. First, when nothing seems to be happening, God is at work behind the scenes.[35] Secondly, while often we appear to be in the hands of others, and feel very much at their disposal, we are in God's hands. Thirdly, God is committed to the preservation of his people. We are his purchased possession — blood-bought.[36] He will never forsake us. Finally, we should rest in God's sovereignty. When we do not understand, we should remind ourselves of what we do know: 'We know that in all things God works for the good of those who love him, who have been called according to his purpose.'[37] The things that we know as Christian believers are greater than the things we do not know! Our peace concerning the future is found in the assurance that our King holds both it and us in his hands.

Troubles were yet ahead of God's people, but triumphs too — and more triumphs than troubles!

3.
Right behaviour and persecution

Please read Esther 3

Chapter 3 begins with a promotion. King Xerxes promoted **'Haman, son of Hammedatha, the Agagite'**, a descendant of Agag, the Amalekite king (3:1).

Relationships between the Israelites and the Amalekites had been bad from an early point in their history. The hostility began in the time of Moses. Moses said, 'The LORD will be at war against the Amalekites from generation to generation,' and Israel was charged with blotting out the memory of Amalek from under heaven.[1] Intermittent conflict with them occurred throughout the Old Testament.[2]

In mentioning Haman's ancestry, the writer of the book of Esther purposely reminds us of one incident in particular recorded in 1 Samuel 15. King Saul, the son of Kish, a Benjamite, was commanded by God to wipe out the Amalekites and to destroy all their property. Instead, in disobedience to God, he spared King Agag as well as the best of their property, with disastrous consequences for Saul and his people. An Amalekite would later claim that he had killed Saul.[3] Israel was still found fighting Amalekites in the days of Hezekiah.[4]

Haman's ancestry is, therefore, mentioned to show that he was an enemy of the Jews by birth, and that it was more than just personal hatred of Mordecai that motivated him.

In effect, Haman became prime minister. First, he was **'honoured'** by the king. Second, he was 'elevated', and, third, literally, the king **'placed his seat above all others that were with him'** (3:1). Promotion can bring out the best or the worst in a person; in Haman's case, it was the latter. Prominence went to his head. The temptation to pride was real. The king even commanded all his officials to bow down and do Haman obeisance (3:2). Haman expected a respect that properly should be given to God alone.

Success does not always come to the deserving, or where we would expect it, whether in the world of sport, the field of battle, employment or human relationships. As the writer of Ecclesiastes says:

> The race is not to the swift
> or the battle to the strong,
> nor does food come to the wise
> or wealth to the brilliant
> or favour to the learned;
> but time and chance happen to them all.[5]

While there must have been some good things to be said in Haman's favour by those who knew him best, his performance in office so far as the Jews were concerned showed him to be deficient of vital human qualities.

Promotion can so easily encourage selfish pride and then bring about a person's downfall. Intoxicated with success and prominence, Haman delighted in the prostration of all and sundry before him at the king's command (3:2).

The picture we gain of Haman is of a man who loved to 'throw his weight about'. Full of his own importance, he delighted in seeing people bow down before him, treating him like the king himself. All the king's subjects that Haman met bowed down, except Mordecai.

Behaviour reveals identity

Our Lord Jesus Christ taught that God's children are identifiable by their behaviour. He spoke of letting our light shine before others so that they may see our good deeds and give praise to our Father in heaven.[6] He underlined that Christian conduct is often in sharp contrast to accepted norms. For example, we are to love those who do not love us, as well as those who do. We are to aim at treating others with the same kindness that characterizes our heavenly Father.[7] Even as a good tree is recognized by its fruit, so Christians are recognizable by their good behaviour.[8] Our Lord's teaching amplifies what Psalm 1:3 says about the truly righteous who may be likened to trees planted by the streams of water, yielding fruit in their season and prospering.

Francis of Assisi is said to have taken one of his young assistants into a nearby town to preach. The young man eagerly anticipated this opportunity to declare the gospel and wondered at what point he would be invited to give his message. Francis led him into the market-place and through the streets, mingling amongst the people. Eventually they returned home. 'But when are we going to preach?' asked the beginner impatiently. Francis then underlined the lesson he wanted to teach. 'We have preached already,' he replied. 'We were observed as we walked. They marked us as we went. It was thus that we preached.' While the young man needed to learn to preach, he needed also to recognize that words carry little weight unless backed up by the unspoken testimony of our lives.

Mordecai's refusal

Behaviour revealed the identity of believers in the fifth century B.C. even as it does today. The incident that sparked off everything happened very quickly. All the king's attendants at court, following the king's instructions, bowed down to Haman and did obeisance. **'But Mordecai would not kneel down or pay him honour'** (3:2). Whatever other contributory factors there were for his refusal, the most basic was his fear of God. Mordecai feared God more than man. He stands out as a practical example of what the fear of God means — a biblical priority. The concluding logic of the book of Ecclesiastes is:

> Now all has been heard;
>> here is the conclusion of the matter:
> Fear God and keep his commandments,
>> for this is the whole duty of man.[9]

Sometimes those who do not profess faith make perceptive observations about biblical concepts. In the post-war years of the twentieth century, a popular BBC Programme was the weekly *Brains Trust*, in which Dr C. E. M. Joad was prominent. He wrote, 'We have abolished the fear of God and instead we live in constant fear of man. We have done away with the idea of hell in the future and we have succeeded in turning our lives in this world into a living hell.'

The fear of the Lord is a constant theme in the book of Psalms, often illustrated.[10] It does not mean that we shun God, but rather that we take refuge in him and seek him. It is the mark of those who genuinely know him, and the root of authentic godliness. It is not a troubled and frightening fear, but a reverential respect in response to his character, and especially his holiness. It shapes our conduct,[11] makes us want to walk in God's ways,[12] and keeps us from sinning.[13] It is the door through which God's wisdom comes to us.[14] The fear of the Lord was the secret of Mordecai's ability to withstand Haman's wrongful demands. Mordecai proved that the fear of the Lord is the secret of a satisfying life, and seeing many good days.[15]

Verse 4 indicates that it was Mordecai's Jewishness that prompted his refusal. The court attendants immediately challenged his negative response: **'Why do you disobey the king's command?'** (3:3). Day by day they continued to challenge him, **'but he refused to comply'**. Clearly Mordecai had explained the reason for his refusal because the narrative indicates that he had told the royal officials that he was a Jew (3:4).

It has been suggested that Mordecai's refusal to bow down to Haman was encouraged by the fact that Haman was a descendant of the long-standing enemies of the Jews, the Agagites (3:1). That makes sense. However, there is no evidence or proof of that motive in the narrative. Plainly the main reason for Mordecai's disobedience was Haman's demand for worship rather than respect. A Jewish Targum says that Haman set up a statue of himself to which everyone was obliged to bow in adoration. To do obeisance to him would have been to break both the first and the second commandments: 'You shall have no other gods before me. You shall not make for yourself an idol in the form of anything in heaven above or on the earth beneath or in the waters below. You shall not bow down to them or worship them.'[16] Worship is God's supreme right, and is not to be given to anyone else. Respect, and even a degree of reverence, may rightly be given to those in authority, but never worship. Haman demanded something God forbids.

Mordecai must have known the probable outcome of his refusal. He was not, however, seeking trouble, but he was aiming to please God. He did not want a confrontation with authority, but he could not deny God's supreme authority. His refusal to justify himself to the royal officials at the king's gate shows him to have been a model of wisdom.[17]

We may sometimes find ourselves with Mordecai's dilemma. Problems of conscience suddenly arise when we are asked to do something we know to be wrong, or second best, or a compromise. Mordecai knew that then — as is still the case — God must be listened to whatever others may say.[18] It is no solution to say, 'Well, everyone compromises nowadays,' or 'If I know which side my bread is buttered, I will conform like the rest.' The only way to peace and a good conscience for a Christian believer is the path of truth and righteousness.

Right behaviour may bring problems

Having established that behaviour reveals the identity of believers, we have to admit that right behaviour sometimes brings misunderstanding and persecution in its wake. The court attendants quickly informed Haman of Mordecai's refusal to bow down and do obeisance on the grounds of his religious principles. They wanted to see if such a refusal would be **'tolerated'** (3:4). The word translated 'be tolerated' literally means 'stand', or 'stand up'. In other words, it was a test case.

When Haman learned of, and then witnessed, Mordecai's refusal, he was furious (3:5). He was not just angry; he became malicious beyond bounds. Not satisfied at the thought of merely destroying Mordecai, he wanted to put an end to all Jews throughout the whole kingdom (3:6). Whether he was aware of it or not, he was intent on breaking the sixth commandment: 'You shall not murder.'[19] He was a fifth-century B.C. anticipation of the twentieth-century A.D. Adolf Hitler.

Persecution was now to be set in motion. The New Testament emphasizes that there is no merit whatsoever in Christians enduring persecution for persecution's sake.[20] We are never to seek or encourage opposition in the mistaken belief that it is automatically to our credit to be persecuted. But, on the other hand, opposition will be the world's frequent response to those who genuinely practise righteousness and godliness.[21]

A people who were different

In looking for a way to remove Mordecai, Haman first re-
sorted to the casting of lots, the guidance of omens, to obtain
direction to select a month and a day to achieve it. He believed in lucky days — as many people sadly still do. He per-
sonally watched as **'they cast the *pur*'** (3:7). Stones or marked
objects were probably thrown together in an urn, shaken to
mix them up together, and then one drawn out to decide the
outcome. Various incantations may have been uttered over
the urn in the process. This practice of casting the lot was
common practice in the East, and was used by the Israelites
themselves when they settled in the land of Canaan.[22] Their
confidence, however, was in God to guide them. Haman's
confidence was elsewhere, like those who put their trust in
horoscopes. The book of Esther provides an illustration of
superstition and its power. The date fixed was a considerable
way ahead, and it gave time for the plan to be communicated
to every part of the empire.

Haman then went to King Xerxes with his complaint and
proposal. **'There is a certain people dispersed and scattered among the peoples in all the provinces of your kingdom whose customs are different from those of all other
people and who do not obey the king's laws; it is not in the
king's best interest to tolerate them. If it pleases the king,
let a decree be issued to destroy them, and I will put ten
thousand talents of silver into the royal treasury for the
men who carry out this business'** (3:8-9). Ten thousand talents was a huge sum, for it represented an attractive fortune
even to a wealthy king. Not knowing the precise identity of
the people whom Haman wanted to exterminate, and certainly
unaware at this stage of Esther's identity with this threatened
race, the king put his seal to Haman's decree of destruction
(3:10).

A **'certain people'** (3:8) can be translated 'one people' and this probably better conveys the way in which Haman made mischievous insinuations. Underlining the fact that the king's empire was made up of many different peoples, of varying races and national backgrounds, he suggested that just one people — a people hardly worth bothering about compared with the many others — were giving trouble. He deliberately withheld their name lest the king should identify individuals whom he knew and respected among them. He was trying to create a prejudice against the whole of the Jewish people on the grounds of one person's actions.

Haman provides a sorry picture of the kind of person whose character God hates:

> There are six things the LORD hates,
>   seven that are detestable to him:
>   haughty eyes,
>   a lying tongue,
>   hands that shed innocent blood,
>   a heart that devises wicked schemes,
>   feet that are quick to rush into evil,
>   a false witness who pours out lies
>   and a man who stirs up dissension among
>   brothers.[23]

Haman was correct in his assessment that the laws and customs of the Jews were **'different from those of all other people'** (3:8). This comment provides a unique picture of the Jews, and their distinctiveness, during the Dispersion. What God did for them at the Exodus was at the heart of their faith and obedience. No doubt their conformity to God's laws made them different in speech, dress and custom. Haman maligned the Jews, however, in accusing them of not keeping the king's laws (3:8). As chapter 2 indicated, Mordecai had proved himself a loyal subject by reporting the conspiracy against the king (see 2:21-23).

The massacre that Haman intended was not without precedent. In 522 B.C. Smerdis the Magus,[24] the son of Cyrus the Great, seized the Persian throne. The Magi seem to have been a priestly caste, or clan, in ancient Persia who served several religions, rather than Zoroastrianism, with which they have often been identified. The Persian Magi were considered to be men of profound wisdom, whereas Babylonian Magi were regarded as impostors. Smerdis the Magus himself was put to death within a year and every Persian took up arms and killed every Magus he could in what came to be called 'the killing of the Magi'. It was only the coming of nightfall that halted the slaughter.

Jews have been the object of people's fury throughout the centuries on account of their obedience to God's laws, given to them as a delivered people, the people of the Exodus. Their laws have been recognized as different from those of others. The suggestion has often been made that it was unprofitable to tolerate them. Their destruction has been attempted through many subtle schemes. They have been misrepresented and then persecuted. Orders have been given to annihilate them. What has been true of the Jewish people has also been true of Christians, and for similar reasons.

Christians, too, must be distinctive

At the heart of Christian experience is the atoning death of our Lord Jesus Christ. It brings the duty and obligation to live no longer for ourselves but for him. Christians possess a similar distinctiveness to the Jews. We too are a delivered, redeemed people.[25] Our spiritual union with our Saviour causes us to begin to share his distinctiveness.

Obedient to his teaching, we render to the state what belongs to it, and to God what belongs to him.[26] If, however, the
state demands what is rightly God's, then we must refuse. When
the state's demands are just and legitimate, there is no conflict, and we are enabled to be exemplary citizens and living
testimonials to the attractive teaching of our Lord Jesus Christ.

We become different, not because we try to be different,
but because the Holy Spirit, who now lives in us, is committed
to making us like our Lord Jesus Christ. 'If the world hates
you,' the Lord Jesus instructed his disciples, 'keep in mind
that it hated me first. If you belonged to the world, it would
love you as its own. As it is, you do not belong to the world,
but I have chosen you out of the world. That is why the world
hates you.'[27]

Obedience to God's laws and moral demands will sometimes make us noticeable, and even conspicuous.[28] Arresting
behaviour will frequently be a key aspect of our testimony.
People will ask, 'Why do you behave in this way?' Then we
have the opportunity to give a reason for the hope we possess.[29] Low standards of morality, whether in industry or in
everyday human relationships, may provide all the greater
opportunity for our lives to shine brightly for Christ.[30] We are
not to expect a fair deal from the world. We should not have a
chip on our shoulder because of hostile attitudes to our witness. Our Lord gave warning that in the world we should have
trouble, but that in him we should have peace. We are to rest
in the assurance that he has overcome the world.[31]

Spiritual conflict

Witness to God as believers involves an ongoing spiritual
struggle with Satan, the god of this world. If we ask who was
behind Haman's malice, the answer is Satan. The promised

Deliverer,[32] the Messiah, was to come through the Jewish race, and so what was more logical than for Satan to try to destroy all the Jews? So far as Satan was concerned, the Jews had to be exterminated because they held the Messianic seed.

Haman's characteristics were those of his spiritual father, the devil.[33] He was proud, insensitive to other people's feelings and convictions, and capable of great anger (3:5). He was like the Bible's description of a fool: 'A fool gives full vent to his anger, but a wise man keeps himself under control.'[34] He was malicious, scheming, untruthful, unscrupulous and callous (3:6,8-9,15). To strengthen his case, he presented the king with a financial incentive — a substantial section of Jewish properties would find their way into the king's treasury. (The twentieth century sadly displayed similar motivation in Europe.) It has been calculated that Haman's bribe amounted to between 58% and 68% of the annual revenue of the Persian Empire.

Everywhere we turn in the Bible we find Satan marked by pride, insensitivity, anger, malice, slyness, lying and callousness. Satan, the enemy of God's people, sees to it, if he can, that the good of God's people is spoken evil of. He even succeeded in causing people to speak evil of our Lord Jesus Christ.[35] It is no surprise, therefore, that he accomplishes the same wickedness against his people. Satan's activity provides no grounds, however, for our not doing what is right in God's sight. The one who is in us is immeasurably greater than the one who is in the world.[36]

'So the king took his signet ring from his finger and gave it to Haman son of Hammedatha, the Agagite, the enemy of the Jews' (3:10), as a symbol of Haman's authority to execute his plan in the king's name. 'Enemy of the Jews' has now become Haman's title, marking his recognized position in the story. He will be called this again.[37]

'**Keep the money,**' the king said to Haman, '**and do with the people as you please**' (3:11). The king said, literally, 'The silver is given to you.' This gives the impression that Xerxes accepted the money as his right, but that he then generously returned it to Haman. Behind this there may be a standard practice in the Middle East of polite refusals that are not genuinely meant. King Xerxes had a reputation for accepting money eagerly. He is said by Herodotus to have melted his money when it came in, and poured it into earthen jars, cutting off solid portions of silver when they were needed.

Persecution is always present somewhere

As we study the Bible and world history, the conclusion becomes inevitable that persecution has always been the lot of God's people somewhere.

Haman's hatred was so great that he instituted a personal vendetta against the whole Jewish community with the most drastic aims: to destroy, slay and annihilate all Jews. '**Then on the thirteenth day of the first month the royal secretaries were summoned. They wrote out in the script of each province and in the language of each people all Haman's orders to the king's satraps, the governors of the various provinces and the nobles of the various peoples**' (3:12). 'Satraps' is an adaptation of a Persian word. They were provincial governors in Persia, of which there were twenty. These orders were written in the name of King Xerxes himself and sealed with his ring. The king's ring gave validity to the documents (see 8:2,8).[38]

'**Dispatches**' were then sent '**by couriers to all the king's provinces**' to achieve the destruction of all Jews — '**young and old, women and little children — on a single day, the**

thirteenth day of the twelfth month, the month of Adar, and to plunder their goods' (3:12-13). Royal decrees were issued in the tongues of all the peoples that coexisted in the Persian Empire (3:12).[39] The variety of languages spoken within it is often emphasized. The date fixed was the day before that on which the Passover lamb was to be slain.[40] It is doubtful if Haman could have been ignorant of this fact. His decision to go ahead with his scheme on this particular date probably, therefore, constituted a deliberate denial on his part of the special providential relationship the Jews had with God. If so, Haman must have been delighted when the lots fell as they did. He probably read it as a confirmation of his gods' approval of his intentions.

The **'couriers'** (3:13) were part of the famous postal service organized by Cyrus, and they were stationed at twenty-four-hour intervals. Haman organized what we know as a 'pogrom' — the Russian word for an organized massacre of a body or class of people. The term 'anti-Semitism' was first coined in Germany in the second part of the nineteenth century, but, as the book of Esther demonstrates, it sadly existed long before that.

Throughout Jewish history — as here in the fifth century B.C., and continuing until the present day — anti-Semitism has reared its ugly head. Between 1903 and 1906, hundreds of Jews were killed, and thousands raped, mutilated and plundered in a series of pogroms in southern Russia, particularly around Kishenev and Odessa. Later, in 1919-1920, the remains of the Ukrainian nationalist army, along with masses of peasants and opportunists, eased their frustrations by murdering some 100,000 of the Jews who came within their reach. The twentieth century was sullied beyond what words can express by anti-Semitic horrors. Hitler's virulent slaughter of Jews meant that one third of the Jews in the world — six million — were wiped out, and millions of others dreadfully tortured.

Haman's goal was nearly realized. There is something tragically pathetic about the final words of chapter 3: **'The king and Haman sat down to drink, but the city of Susa was bewildered'** (3:15). It implies that the population in general was confused, and perhaps even that the ordinary people lamented and grieved over what was happening. Generally speaking, the Persians were not intolerant of the Jews, and nowhere in the book of Esther does any antagonism towards them appear apart from Haman and those who supported him. The statement that the king and Haman 'sat down to drink' (3:15) is another way of saying that they feasted, while others had sorrow inflicted upon them.

The Christian church has probably been persecuted at every stage of her history somewhere in the world. Just as we may draw a world map marking areas where wars take place, so we could draw one indicating areas where obvious persecution against Christians occurs. It has been estimated that something like 330,000 Christians are martyred for their faith each year.[41] We could similarly mark the map showing the areas where persecution exists, although in a less blatant form.

Happily, however, history, like the book of Esther, is the story of God's vindication of his people. Four helpful conclusions may be drawn from this chapter.

First, an old saying: *'There is nothing new under the sun.'*[42] While we sometimes feel we are unique in our situations and challenges, we are not. We follow in a noble tradition. One of the benefits of reading the Bible, as with the study of history, is the realization that little has really changed in the world, and men and women scarcely at all.

Secondly, we have an important reminder that *there is a battle going on in the world, and in the universe itself.* It is a conflict between light and darkness, between God and Satan. It is all the more difficult a battle because so much of it is unseen, and is fought in the heavenly realms.[43] It revolves around the gospel of our Lord Jesus Christ, and its progress. That was what the conflict was about even here in the book of Esther. If the Jews could have been totally exterminated, then God's promises could not have found their fulfilment in a Jewish virgin's giving birth to the Messiah. Nothing is more important than the gospel of our Lord Jesus Christ. It is around his gospel that the spiritual warfare in the world still focuses.

Thirdly, we have *a stimulus to pray.* For us there is perhaps little immediate cost to our discipleship in terms of persecution. But that is not the case in many other parts of the world. The cry of our fellow Christians in those places is, 'Pray for us!'[44]

Finally, we have *a challenge as to how we live our lives in an unbelieving world.* Are we prepared to be different because of our obedience to God's laws and our discipleship of our Lord Jesus Christ?

4.
The secret of courage

Please read Esther 4

'Jews everywhere in peril!' Such a banner headline in a news-paper could have summarized the situation of Jews through-out the Persian Empire, as we find it described in chapter 3. At the heart of the problem is the manner in which King Xerxes had singled out Haman, an Agagite, for promotion as his prime minister.

'What shall I do?'

Chapter 4 begins with Mordecai's discovery of what was afoot (4:1). We do not know how he heard of the transactions that lay behind the formal edict. Perhaps friends at court, or his opportunities of hearing snippets of news at the king's gate (2:21-22), or the eunuchs of the Persian court, who were every-where, provided him with the information. We are not told what his thought processes were as he undoubtedly asked him-self, 'What shall I do?' Perhaps, more important still, he asked God, 'What do you want me to do?' Whatever went on in his mind, Mordecai came to see that God's answer could well rest with the remarkable position that God had given to Esther.

Whenever difficult or frightening things take place, there is usually some indication of God's forward planning on our behalf. There is always some 'way out'[1] — although that escape route may come through an infinite variety of God-ordained means.

A public demonstration

Mordecai's first problem was how to get in touch with Esther. His solution was a public demonstration with one person in mind (4:1-9). There is truth in the popular proverb, 'Where there is a will, there is a way.' Mordecai acted in a somewhat dramatic manner: he tore his garments and put on sackcloth and ashes (4:1). The use of sackcloth and ashes to express grief or to acknowledge guilt was common practice. **'Sack-cloth'** describes the rough hair (in the East commonly camel's hair) from which sacks or coarser garments were made, worn by the poorest people, or by mourners. To clothe oneself with sackcloth was to assume the recognized symbol of mourning. The people of Nineveh did this when Jonah delivered God's judgement to them.[2] **'Ashes'** were a similar symbol.

Having so dressed himself, Mordecai went through the whole city, **'wailing loudly and bitterly'**, until he arrived at **'the king's gate'** (4:1-2). This gate was not simply one among many entrances to the city, but the door to the palace itself. No one dressed in sackcloth was allowed to enter the palace, for such garments made individuals ceremonially unclean, and unfit for the king's presence.

The sackcloth and ashes, when no bereavement had taken place, and the public nature of Mordecai's behaviour were calculated to attract Esther's serious attention. Mordecai knew it would not be long before the news of his conduct and actions would be reported all around the palace, and would reach Esther's ears.

Associated with this motive of catching Esther's attention, there may well have been Mordecai's intense sorrow that it had been an action of his — his not bowing down to Haman — that had sparked off such violent hostility to his people. The gravest possible danger and misfortune threatened his whole race because of his simple refusal to break God's commandments. Never before since the events surrounding the Exodus had the Jews been in such danger.

Mordecai's initiative was effective. When Queen Esther's maids and eunuchs went and told her, she was overcome with grief (4:4). She sent clothes to Mordecai for him to put on in place of his sackcloth, but he refused them. Probably his refusal was calculated to indicate to Esther that the sorrow he was expressing was not a small personal matter, but something that concerned his whole people.

The result was that Esther sent out Hathach, a eunuch whom the king had appointed to wait on her, to discover the cause of Mordecai's mourning (4:5). Mordecai told him what had happened, and about the sum of money Haman had offered to pay into the royal treasury as compensation for the destruction of the Jews (4:6-7). He also gave him a copy of the edict of extermination, published in Susa, for him to show Esther. With it went the message that she should go to the king and implore his favour and **'plead with him for her people'** (4:8). The mention of **'the text of the edict'** being shown to Esther indicates that she was literate. The word **'urge'** (4:8) comes from a Hebrew verb, *'sawa'*, that means to command or to charge in an authoritative sense. **'Hathach went back and reported to Esther what Mordecai had said'** (4:9). Mordecai's first objective had been achieved.

God's sovereignty

The book of Esther is about God's sovereignty and providence, and the certainty of his intervention on his people's behalf. That certainty, however, does not preclude action and initiative on our part. God may be behind the initiative we take. John Calvin recognized that God's providence is no reason to put aside our human responsibility for action: 'We are not at all hindered by God's eternal decrees either from looking ahead for ourselves or from putting all our affairs in order, but always in submission to his will... It is very clear what our duty is: thus, if the Lord has committed to us the protection of our life, our duty is to protect it; if he offers helps, to use them; if he forewarns us of dangers, not to plunge headlong; if he makes remedies available, not to neglect them.'[3]

When we are most aware of our struggle against Satan and his dark forces, it is not a time for sitting back, or abandoning ourselves to pessimism or despair. Rather, we must renew our dependence upon God, striving to put on 'the full armour' he provides,[4] and then ask, 'What would the Lord have us do?' Our assurance of God's sovereignty is no excuse for failing to do our duty, whether in missions, evangelism or the building up of the church of our Lord Jesus Christ. The friends and colleagues of William Carey, the pioneer missionary, presented him with innumerable obstacles when he first suggested going to India. Some even went so far as to put forward the idea that if God wanted the people of India brought to faith in our Lord Jesus Christ, he would accomplish it without their endeavours. Carey rightly responded by reminding them of our Lord Jesus' final command to his church. Later on in his life, as he looked back, he said, 'Few people know what *may* be done until they *try*, and *persevere* in what they undertake.'

An initial hesitancy

Mordecai's instructions met with a faint-hearted yet honest response (4:10-11). We can imagine the overwhelming sense of responsibility and inadequacy that Esther felt. She replied to Mordecai that his request seemed almost impossible to achieve. If anyone approached the king in the inner court without being summoned there was only one penalty — death.

The **'inner court'** (4:11) seems to have been the entrance hall of an impressive apartment in the more private residence of the king, where he met with his councillors for the transaction of state business. Seated on his throne at the upper end of the apartment, he could see any person in the court. The only exemption from death was if the king, by pointing his golden sceptre towards that individual, granted that person his or her life (4:11).

All four occurrences of the use of this word for **'sceptre'** are found in the book of Esther.[5] The Persian sceptre consisted of golden rods bound together. Laws established by Dioces the Mede, and enforced by the Persian monarchs, forbade any approach to the king without a summons.[6] Individuals looked for the nod of this golden stick.

The intention behind this rule was the protection of the king's life, time and privacy. Josephus adds the interesting note that 'Round his throne stood men with axes to punish any who approached the throne without being summoned.' The wisdom of the advice of the book of Proverbs was timely:

Do not exalt yourself in the king's presence,
    and do not claim a place among great men;
it is better for him to say to you, 'Come up here,'
    than for him to humiliate you before a nobleman. [7]

How different is our King! How welcome we are to come to him![8] One of the glorious benefits of our reconciliation to God is our access to him.[9] Peace with God and access to him go hand in hand.[10]

Esther also informed Mordecai that she had not been called into the king's presence for thirty days (4:11). This perhaps implied that she thought she was out of favour with the king, a factor that served to increase the difficulty of her making any approach to him.

While Esther emerges as something of a heroine, she was made of the same stuff as we are, with a natural proneness for seeing the difficulties rather than anticipating what God could, and would, do. It is a great encouragement to appreciate that those men and women whom God has used in the past had the same emotions and failings as we do.[11]

Faint-heartedness is a natural reaction to challenging situations, but it is not a spiritual reaction. Cowardice is one of the most common and yet least conspicuous sins. Sometimes we may be faint-hearted in our *attitudes*. We perhaps never really grapple with vital and important issues because we are fearful of our ability to handle them. We may be faint-hearted in our *actions*, acting hesitantly instead of boldly. We may be faint-hearted in our *prayers*, never rising to the truth that God is able to do exceeding abundantly above all that we can ask or imagine.[12] Boldness of faith should characterize us first in prayer, and then in the action that faith in God demands.[13]

To the point

Mordecai's response to Esther was short and sharp! He was utterly realistic: **'Do not think that because you are in the king's house you alone of all the Jews will escape'** (4:13). He was also forthright and blunt: **'For if you remain silent at this time, relief and deliverance for the Jews will arise from another place, but you and your father's family will perish. And who knows but that you have come to royal position for such a time as this?'** (4:14).

'Another place' (4:14) may be interpreted in different ways. 'Place' can mean 'sanctuary', or God's dwelling in heaven. In a number of places God is said to assist men and women from his heavenly abode.[14] Zechariah urges, 'Be still before the LORD, all mankind, because he has roused himself from his holy dwelling.'[15] Jews sang Psalm 33, with its testimony:

> From heaven the LORD looks down
>   and sees all mankind;
> from his dwelling-place he watches
>   all who live on earth —
> he who forms the hearts of all,
>   who considers everything they do.
> No king is saved by the size of his army;
>   no warrior escapes by his great strength.
> A horse is a vain hope for deliverance;
>   despite all its great strength it cannot save.
> But the eyes of the LORD are on those who fear him,
>   on those whose hope is in his unfailing love,
> to deliver them from death
>   and keep them alive in famine.[16]

'Another' can also bear the sense of 'unusual' or 'strange'. Believing Jews knew that their help came uniquely from the Lord who made the heaven and the earth.[17] Josephus suggests that 'another place' is a substitute for God's name.[18]

Mordecai's measured reply was intended to remind Esther that it was more important to fear God than people, and that she should not forget the reassuring truth of God's providential care and rule (4:14). 'He who watches over Israel will neither slumber nor sleep.'[19] Esther's initial reply had been dictated more by fear of the king than fear of God.

There are times when it is inappropriate to be silent, and to say nothing is a sin worthy of judgement. Influence is always to be exercised in the interests of righteousness. Priceless opportunities may be given to us any day without warning.

When we pray daily, as we are encouraged to do, 'Your king-dom come,' we must expect unique moments to arise for in-fluencing others for good, and we must seize them.

Human responsibility and divine providence are wonder-fully integrated.[20] Opportunities for accomplishing God's will are given to us, but if we reject or neglect them, others will be given the privilege, to their profit and our loss.[21] God's pur-poses are much greater than the obedience or disobedience of one person. We are all where we are in God's purpose — in our work, families and churches. God's sovereignty is a truth to reckon upon always:

> The LORD works out everything for his own ends —
>   even the wicked for a day of disaster...
> In his heart a man plans his course,
>   but the LORD determines his steps.[22]

Perhaps there is something here for us to take note of as we think of the influence we all exercise in our homes, our place of work and our church fellowship. When crises occur, we cannot opt out and pretend they do not concern us. Some-times it is right and wise to keep quiet, but on other occasions the only right thing to do is to speak. Whatever we do, our keeping silence or our speaking out is not to be influenced by fear of what people may think, say or do, but rather by our reverence for God. Our Saviour said, 'For whoever wants to save his life will lose it, but whoever loses his life for me will find it.'[23]

We sometimes need to be extremely forthright in exhorting one another to do the right thing, just as Mordecai did with Esther. Our best friends are those who love us enough to be genuinely honest with us.[24] Sometimes rebuke is appropriate, as it was here in the book of Esther, and centuries later in the life of the apostle Peter when Paul rebuked him to his face

because of his wrong behaviour towards Gentile Christians.[25]
When relationships are good, reprimands can be given, even
welcomed, and accepted in the spirit in which they are given.

A right response

Mordecai's forthrightness produced the right result because
Esther responded with courageous determination (4:15-17).
We find it expressed in verse 16: **'And if I perish, I perish.'**
These were not so much words of pessimism but of resolution,
backed by at least four factors which we may identify.

1. Esther knew that she could not hope to escape the threatened destruction

She had to face the facts of the situation. Her first reaction,
though understandable, had not been the right one.

God has bound his people together. The relationship we
have to one another in his family, and in his Son's church, is
very precious, but it brings great responsibility. There are duties
we cannot escape if we want to serve God, and do his will.

Our Lord Jesus Christ is our example here, as elsewhere.
Death's destruction is what his people deserve for their sins.
Our Lord Jesus, however, had no sin, and his life was in every
way a perfect life, completely acceptable to his Father. But
our Lord's identity with his people meant that their destruction had to be his. This was no small thing for the Son of God
whose fellowship with the Father had never once been impaired or broken. In the Garden of Gethsemane he shrank from
the cross as he contemplated its agony, knowing how desperate and desolating was the experience he faced of bearing the
sins of all his people. But his cry was: 'Father, if you are willing, take this cup from me; yet not my will, but yours be done.'[26]

The Lord Jesus would have us freely identify ourselves with his people, whatever the cost. That is an aspect and part of our filling up in our flesh 'what is still lacking in regard to Christ's afflictions, for the sake of his body, which is the church'.[27]

2. Esther could not live just for herself

Like us, she was a private individual, with her life to live, but also like us, she was inevitably joined with others in the bundle of life. Whether it was always congenial or not, Esther had responsibility for others. As private individuals, we all have our own personalities and way to make in life. Having said that, the life of each of us has an impact upon others, and we are responsible for that impact. We feel this responsibility all the more as Christians since our Lord Jesus died and rose again that he might be our Lord, and that we might no longer live for ourselves but for him.[28] As Christians, we are members of the one body, the one flock and the one family of God. We cannot live, therefore, just for ourselves. Our actions must have the good of others in view. Our determination must be to live wholeheartedly and unreservedly for our Lord Jesus. As his concern was not to live and die for himself but for others, so our concern must be the same.

3. Esther knew there could be no doubt about God's providence in bringing her to such prominence in Persia

Mordecai's question had the frightening stab of reality: **'Who knows but that you have come to royal position for such a time as this?'** (4:14). Mordecai clearly believed in an over-ruling providence. When we pray, we find that 'coincidences' happen. In what we call 'coincidences' we may often be witnessing God's control of history. Mordecai suggested that there was more than coincidence involved in Esther's exaltation. She must often have pondered the strange course of events that had led to her coronation. Maybe she had wondered, 'Why me?' Perhaps now she began to see the answer to her question. 'We should, every one of us, consider for what end God has put us in the place where we are. And when an opportunity arises to serve God and our generation, we must take care not to let it slip.'[29]

The sure and perfect outworking of God's will in human lives is beyond doubt. God controls the course of history, even down to the moment of our birth. When God sent his own Son into the world, it was not a minute too late or a minute too early. It was when the appointed time came that God sent his Son into the world.[30] At the moment it occurred, the world saw no significance in it, but it changed not only the calendar, but also the whole direction of human history.

While the outworking of God's providence in our lives may not be anything like as dramatic as it was either in Esther's life or in the coming of our Saviour into the world, it is just as certain and careful. God has plans for our lives.[31] Those plans extend to where we live, our place of work, our relationships and our gifts for service in the body of Christ.

There is a sense in which God's servants have all been born 'for such a time as this'. We should all be asking (whether we are young like Esther, or older like Mordecai), 'What work has God especially for me to do because he has allowed me to be alive at this particular time?'

What a tragedy if God has to pass us over and use other people because of our unreadiness! (4:14). We are given the privilege of being part of God's plans, but our failure cannot thwart his sovereign purposes. Sometimes Christians spend time lamenting the days in which they live because they imagine that the difficulties of contemporary life are greater than those in which earlier believers lived. Whatever may be the truth about any such comparisons, we ought rather to praise God for the privilege of living today, and determine to fulfil the good works for which we have been 'twice born'.[32]

4. Esther knew that the most important thing to do was to express her dependence upon God

Her reply to Mordecai's instructions was: **'Go, gather together all the Jews who are in Susa, and fast for me. Do not eat or drink for three days, night or day. I and my maids will fast as you do. When this is done, I will go to the king, even though it is against the law. And if I perish, I perish'** (4:16).

From this point on Esther took the initiative. She determined to go to the king illegally, disobeying the law even as Mordecai had done earlier. She recognized that there was a higher power whose laws she was to obey. She acknowledged the possibility of failure, but she had the hope of success. Although prayer is not mentioned, it is implied. The reference to her 'maids' (4:16) seems to indicate that she had surrounded herself with Jewish girls who would willingly join her in fasting and prayer. Her statement tells us what she did not trust in: she did not place her confidence in her own beauty, position or eloquence. To fast could well have detracted from her beauty. The mention of fasting indicates where Esther placed her trust.

Old Testament law did not particularly command fasting, except on the Day of Atonement.[33] It was not therefore regarded as obligatory. It was seen to have no merit in and of itself, in that it could become merely an outward act of no spiritual value, as when Jezebel proclaimed a fast with the motive of obtaining Naboth's vineyard for Ahab.[34]

Fasting was the regular accompaniment of prayer. Nehemiah's reaction on hearing bad news that only God could remedy was: 'When I heard these things, I sat down and wept.

For some days I mourned and fasted and prayed before the God of heaven.'[35] Prayer is the principal purpose of fasting, in that fasting concentrates the mind and helps to detach it from current preoccupations. Fasting itself was perceived as a form of prayer.[36]

Fasting, therefore, is a way of abstaining from what may interfere with prayer. It is an expression of earnestness, and recognition of the seriousness of a situation, expressing either sorrow[37] or repentance.[38] This is appropriate, since sorrow tends to destroy the desire for food. Abstaining from food for a while has the potential for sharpening our spiritual sensibilities, and bringing us into a closer fellowship with what is unseen and eternal. It is a deliberate act of discipline in order to concentrate upon prayer and to express serious dependence upon God. Our minds are less inclined to act when our bodies are full of food.

The Pharisees fasted, as did John the Baptist's disciples.[39] Our Lord Jesus fasted for forty days and forty nights before beginning his public ministry.[40] He did not condemn fasting, but he did condemn the pride that could lie behind it. The fasting that God particularly rewards is done in secret, as an activity directed towards him and not our fellow men and women.[41] The Lord Jesus taught that it must never be seen as a substitute for a proper heart-relationship to God.[42] When questioned about fasting, he indicated that it is more part of the old order of things than the new order that he introduced.[43]

The early church backed up prayer with fasting[44] as an expression of earnestness. It was in the context of prayer and fasting that important decisions were made, such as the setting apart of missionaries for their spheres of service.

Calvin recommended fasting to the church and to the individual Christian as an occasional exercise in order to acknowledge with humility the rightness of God's judgements and to apprehend God more clearly and immediately in prayer. He was careful, however, to warn against regarding it as 'meritorious work or a kind of divine worship'.[45]

One of our great difficulties as fallen human beings is to keep things in balance, and not to go to extremes. Charles Simeon, the eighteenth-century Cambridge preacher, at the age of sixty-eight, was asked whether his self-discipline extended to fasting. His answer was: 'In former years I derived much personal benefit from fasting; but now I cannot, for I should disable myself from my needful duties, as it would impair my little strength.'[46]

With similar wise concern for physical well-being, Samuel Rutherford wrote to a friend, 'Remember you are in the body, and it is the lodging-house; and you may not, without offending the Lord, suffer the old walls of that house to fall down through want of necessary food... It is a fearful sin in us, by hurting the body by fasting, to loose one stone, or the least piece of timber in it, for the house is not your own.'[47]

J. A. Haldane, a Scottish evangelist of the same era as Simeon, linked fasting with prayer. Whenever there was any subject or issue in which he particularly needed God's counsel and wisdom, he made a habit of setting apart a day for the purpose of humbling himself and making known his requests to God.[48] It was with this purpose in view that Esther did the same.

Esther was wise to recognize that the best preparation for individual action, and corporate action, is to express dependence upon God. 'It is better to take refuge in the LORD than to trust in princes.'[49] None can measure the value of covenanting together to pray. The intensity and reality of corporate prayer may be aided immeasurably by fasting (4:16-17). J. Oswald Saunders, one-time Overseas Director of the Overseas Missionary Fellowship, formerly the China Inland Mission, wrote in the mission's magazine, 'In the history of the China Inland Mission the tide in many a crisis has turned when its workers have met the situation with prayer and fasting. Many a stubborn city has opened, many an intransigent heart has yielded, many a financial need has been resolved by this means.'

In effect, Esther asked the Jewish community to intercede for her. While her natural fearfulness probably remained, she exchanged faint-heartedness for courage as she gave expression to her trust in God. She and her fellow-Jews had every reason to do so because of God's declared commitment to them and faithfulness to his promises. 'When you are in distress and all these things have happened to you, then in later days you will return to the LORD your God and obey him. For the LORD your God is a merciful God; he will not abandon or destroy you or forget the covenant with your forefathers, which he confirmed to them by oath.'[50] Upon such promises Esther and her people now relied.

It is an abiding principle that 'Those who hope in the LORD will renew their strength.'[51] We referred earlier to our Lord Jesus in the Garden of Gethsemane facing the prospect of the cross in all its bitterness. As he surrendered his will to his Father's, the Father sent an angel to strengthen him.[52]

Fearfulness is understandable, but it is never a legitimate excuse for neglect of duty, since the Lord is the Saviour and the strength of his people. 'God did not give us a spirit of timidity, but a spirit of power, of love and of self-discipline.'[53] God calls us to be courageous rather than faint-hearted.[54]

We are to recognize God's providence in our lives, and live in step with our understanding of his will. We are to express our dependence upon him with earnestness every time our faith is challenged. To all of these things God calls us, as he did Esther.

It is an interesting exercise to contrast the important events in the book of Esther associated, on the one hand, with feasting and drinking[55] and those, on the other hand, with fasting.[56] As we do so, there is no doubt what the proper attitude of

God's believing people should be as they ask for God's help and direction.

'So Mordecai went away ...' (4:17). 'Went away' is literally 'passed over' or 'crossed over', which seems to indicate that he crossed a river. The Kharkha River separated the fortress from Susa. He went away **'and carried out all of Esther's instructions'** (4:17). Esther is now to the fore. For such a time and such an initiative God had been preparing her from birth. [57]

5.
The way up and
the way down

Please read Esther 5

The way up often proves to be the way down, and the way
down the way up! One of life's paradoxes, that truth is illustrated by the dramatic events of this chapter. Haman, the villain in the narrative, full of pride, sought to advance only himself and his self-interest. God brought him down. Esther, on
the other hand, humbled herself, and expressed it by fasting
and prayer. God raised her up to amazing usefulness and permanent renown.

Who holds our life in his hands?

In considering these two principal characters in this chapter,
we begin with Esther. 'If I perish, I perish,' had been her message to Mordecai when she promised to obey his instructions
and seek an audience with the king (4:16).

Esther was under no illusions as to the risk she was taking,
from the human point of view (4:11). We shall understand the
narrative better if we try to enter into her feelings. The king —
like any oriental monarch — had supreme authority. In his
hands were life and death for his subjects. To appear uninvited
before him was to ignore the required code of behaviour. Some
might have said that Esther was playing with her life.

It prompts the question: 'Who really holds our life in his hands?' The Bible's answer is: 'God does.' This assurance, however, is not an invitation to stupidity and abandonment of common sense. Satan, for example, encouraged our Lord Jesus Christ to throw himself down from the parapet of the temple, quoting God's promise that he would put his servant in the charge of his angels, who would protect him against all dangers.[1] Our Lord immediately rejected this temptation because it was a misapplication of Scripture and constituted a wrong approach to trust in God's protection. However, God does have the lives of all his servants in his care. We may have confidence to say to him, 'My times are in your hands.'[2] We shall not die a moment before God appoints or allows. While King Xerxes wore the crown of Persia, the Lord, to whom Esther committed herself, is the everlasting Sovereign, who has given us his Son as our King.

The contrast between our Saviour's crown and kingdom and those of Xerxes is immense. Xerxes, having on one occasion reviewed his army, initiated a rowing match, which the Phoenicians of Sidon won. Afterwards, his uncle Artabanus was surprised to find Xerxes weeping. He asked the reason. 'I was thinking,' Xerxes replied, 'and it came into my mind how pitifully short human life is — for of all these thousands of men not one will be alive in a hundred years' time.'[3] Xerxes also had a dream of world dominion in which, having imagined himself crowned as king over all the earth, he then suddenly saw the crown disappear from his head.'[4] His nightmare came true in 465 B.C. when the officers of his palace assassinated him. The crown, however, of our Saviour Jesus Christ is 'resplendent'.[5] The word translated 'resplendent' literally means, 'will flourish'. His glories as King will never fade. His kingdom cannot fail. Innumerable crowns have been placed upon the heads of sovereigns throughout the centuries. Some consisted of laurels and ivy. They have all withered, decayed and perished. Our Saviour's crown never decays. Rather, it blossoms. We never have to use the past tense of his kingship.

Some of the anxieties and fretfulness of daily life spring from feeling that our lives and destinies are, to some extent at least, in the hands of others. But that is not ultimately the case. It is true that others may have some control over us — and often legitimately so — but only in so far as God permits.

The most obvious example, for our encouragement, is our Lord Jesus Christ himself as he was handed over to Jewish and Roman authorities at the time of his trial and execution. As in our imagination we watch him being buffeted, spat upon and brutally treated, he appears helpless. Standing before Pilate, he seems powerless. But the opposite was the case! He was in his Father's hands. The Father was taking him to the cross. The Father was going to turn the greatest evil into the greatest good for our eternal salvation. Significantly, it was into his Father's hands that the Lord Jesus committed his spirit as he died.[6]

Esther's life, too, was in God's hands as she dressed herself in her full splendour as queen on the third day (5:1). What a glorious assurance it is to know that our future, and all it contains, is in God's perfect control! That is a confidence we may have, not only for ourselves, but also for all whom we love and for whom we are concerned.

Wisdom from heaven

Esther acted with great wisdom — with 'the wisdom from above',[7] given to those who genuinely seek it when trials come.[8] To give wisdom is the prerogative of the Lord in whose hands our lives are. He is 'magnificent in wisdom'.[9]

Esther's action recorded in this chapter followed three days of fasting and prayer. 'Lord, please give me wisdom,' must have been at the heart of her prayers and those of all who prayed for her (4:16). It delights God when his children seek his fatherly wisdom and counsel. Most, if not all, of our mistakes arise from our failure to do so.

Esther first reminded the king that she was his queen by putting on **'her royal robes'** (5:1). Literally the Hebrew reads, she 'put on her royalty'. She put on not merely attractive clothes, but royal apparel that Xerxes himself must have bestowed upon her earlier. She then made her entry to the king. He was seated **'on his royal throne'** (5:1). When he saw her standing in the court, **'He was pleased with her and held out to her the gold sceptre that was in his hand'** (5:2). When the king extended the golden sceptre to an individual it was a sign of royal pardon, and the annulling of the death sentence that had been incurred in making an unauthorized approach to him. 'When a king's face brightens, it means life; his favour is like a rain cloud in spring.'[10] This was the first part of God's answer to her prayers and the intercession of those supporting her in her action.

The king was generous in his response: **'What is it, Queen Esther? What is your request? Even up to half the kingdom, it will be given you'** (5:3). Kings were in the habit of making exaggerated and outrageous promises. King Herod did the same in the first century when he said to Herodias' daughter, Salome, 'Whatever you ask I will give you, up to half my kingdom.'[11] Esther must have been greatly encouraged at the king's reaction. Her prayers were being answered in a way that was immeasurably greater than all she could have asked or imagined.[12] So often we find that our fears and apprehensions have been unnecessary because God has gone before us. This passage needs to be read against the background of the principle stated in Proverbs 21:1: 'The king's heart is in the hand of the LORD; he directs it like a water-course wherever he pleases.'[13]

Esther's immediate response to the king's invitation was a simple request that he and Haman should come to a dinner she had prepared that day for the king (5:4). We may perhaps be surprised at what appear to be Esther's delaying tactics, but she had sought to discover from God the right moment to make her urgent request, and she now worked towards it. When we strive to do God's will in dependence upon him, there are moments — difficult to explain or define — when we simply feel it right to wait, or to delay the action we know we must take at some point.

When the time arrived for the dinner, the king repeated his willingness to meet almost any request of Esther's (5:6). Her reply was to promise to tell the king what she wanted if he and Haman would come again to dinner the next day (5:7-8). Besides displaying modesty, she also indicated that the request she wanted to make was something exceptional.

We cannot be sure of Esther's motive in inviting Haman. It was, however, entirely appropriate in view of his premiership. It certainly served to give him a false sense of security and averted suspicion on his part that something affecting him was afoot. Esther had a plan in mind, and she was setting a well-designed trap for Haman.

We must remember throughout this narrative that Esther had sought God's guidance, and she followed, therefore, the direction he gave her as she did what seemed best. Dependent upon God as she was, she knew she had her part to play.

We must not forget either what was going on behind the scenes. The background to this encouraging start was the unseen prayers and fasting of Mordecai and his fellow Jews. What was happening for the good of God's people was influenced as much by their hidden activity as by Esther's more public action (4:17). Our prayers likewise may bring fresh courage

and strength to God's servants in strategic and often dangerous situations. God has the whole world in his hands, and it is
to him we pray, calling him 'our Father'.

Pride's downfall

We turn now to Haman's involvement in the events of this
chapter. For Esther the way down is proving the way up. But
the reverse is to be the case for Haman. There is more hope
for a fool than for someone like Haman who is 'wise in his
own eyes'.[14]

'Haman went out that day happy and in high spirits'
(5:9). It is appropriate to place an emphasis upon *that day*
because it was to be the last day that he knew such joy and
happiness. The knowledge that he was to be the sole guest of
both the king and queen at a prestigious banquet filled him
with considerable pleasure. His delight increased when he was
invited for the second time the following day, with the prospect of hearing the queen's special request to the king (5:7-8).
We can imagine him thinking, 'Won't my wife and friends be
impressed and jealous! Who would not want to be Prime Minister of Persia?' And so it was that Haman left the palace full
of joy and high spirits. He was walking on air as he returned
home. Human happiness may often be built upon such false
hopes and shaky foundations.

The fly in the ointment

Just one thing spoiled Haman's happiness. It was the presence
of Mordecai at the king's gate. It was not the mere sight of
Mordecai that aroused Haman's anger, but the sight of him in
his capacity as a royal official. As Haman passed by him,

Mordecai neither stood up, nor stirred himself at his approach. Haman felt a great gust of anger. However, he restrained himself. His plans, already set in motion, were going to destroy Mordecai — or so he thought. His pride was hurt, but he looked forward to Mordecai's permanent removal (5:9-10). Esther's strategy had succeeded in lulling Haman into a false sense of security.

Haman's pride, however, had its full fling when he arrived home. He gathered together his wife Zeresh and his friends (5:10), and with boundless arrogance held forth about his dazzling wealth, his many children, how the king had raised him to a position of honour and promoted him over the heads of the king's administrators and ministers (5:11).[15]

Pride, sadly, delights in comparisons. It takes special pleasure in unique honours or supposed superiority. Roy Plomley, the originator and first presenter of the BBC's *Desert Island Discs* programme, offered his guests a conducted tour of Broadcasting House if they had not visited it before. He took them to see the library index, an impressive sight, for it contained the catalogue of a million discs, with each item listed by title, composer and artist. On one occasion he took the operatic tenor Nicolai Gedda to see the index. 'He had made his first record within a fortnight of his debut, at Stockholm Opera House, and he was delighted to see how thick was the bunch of index cards bearing his name. He then ran to the drawer containing the cards of his great rival, the Italian Franco Corelli, and measured his cards against Corelli's. "I'm thicker than Franco!" he shouted happily.'[16] Such is the character of human pride. The Greek word for 'pride' means 'one who shows himself above other people'. In the Shipibos language of Peru, 'pride' is translated as, 'I outrank others.'

Pride usually focuses upon wealth, family, promotion or honour, and finds its freest expression by means of the tongue. Haman is typical of the person whose total preoccupation is with all that this present world offers, with its pride in prestige and possessions.[17]

How proud are we of our wealth, family, promotion or prominence? Do we speak or act with regard to these benefits forgetting that they are God's gifts to us? Pride is one of the greatest sins because it makes us treat God's gifts as if they rightfully belonged to us, and were created by us. Our pride robs God of his right to be acknowledged as the source of all the good we know and enjoy. As in the case of Haman, pride finds its freest expression in our words. While one of the smallest parts of our body, the tongue can do the most damage, like a forest fire.[18]

Pride's gallows

'Pride goes before destruction, a haughty spirit before a fall.'[19] In all exhibitions of pride there are the seeds of its downfall, as Haman illustrates. Having shared everything of which he was proud, Haman capped it all by telling his family and friends that Queen Esther had invited the king and no one else apart from himself to a repeat banquet the next day (5:12). Then he opened his heart: **'But all this gives me no satisfaction as long as I see that Jew Mordecai sitting at the king's gate'** (5:13). Fallen humanity is never satisfied. Haman's misery arose from his most prominent vice — his pride. He demonstrates how God's judgement upon sin is not only future, but also to some extent present. He is an example of those on the broad road that leads to destruction, and typical of those we might imagine as being happy in the world. To all outward appearances, they seem to have 'made it' and to possess everything. We may be unaware, however, of the foolish and petty things that secretly bother them.

God has built the principle into human life that 'Misfortune pursues the sinner, but prosperity is the reward of the righteous,' although this may not be seen immediately, as so often the wicked seem to prosper.[20] The possession of the king's favour, his family's admiration, his wealth and his position — none of this satisfied Haman so long as one Jew refused to give him the respect he demanded. Pride and resentment go hand in hand. To allow pride to fill the heart is to find it easy to want revenge. It is to lose the enjoyment of life through little things that offend us.

His wife Zeresh and his friends came up with a suggestion: **'Have a gallows built, seventy-five feet high, and ask the king in the morning to have Mordecai hanged on it. Then go with the king to the dinner and be happy'** (5:14). A height of seventy-five feet was calculated to make the structure extremely prominent. Haman's friends recognized the blow Mordecai had given his pride. They would, however, have been better friends to him if they had warned him of the danger of his wounded pride and where it would lead him.[21] Their evil suggestion pleased Haman more than all his wealth and prestige.[22] Delighted with the advice, Haman had the gallows erected.

The Bible clearly establishes that 'God opposes the proud, but gives grace to the humble.'[23] And, of course, his opposition is entirely appropriate. Our pride is a form of dishonesty since it gives us false views of our own importance. It is frequently the substitution and exaltation of ourselves in the place of God. It allies us to Satan. 'Oh, that I could always see myself in my proper colours!' wrote George Whitefield as a young man. 'I believe I should have little reason to fall down and worship myself. God be merciful to me a sinner!'

The example of our Lord Jesus Christ

The best antidote to pride is the development of our Lord Jesus Christ's attitudes in us.[24] When we treat one another after the pattern of his example, there is no unhealthy competition between us, no conceit, and we strive to be self-effacing. We then consider others to be better than ourselves, and place their interests before our own.[25]

Our Lord Jesus Christ demonstrated that the way down is the way up. He humbled himself and became a man. He assumed the condition of a slave, and accepted even death upon a cross. But God the Father raised him high, and 'seated him at his right hand in the heavenly realms, far above all rule and authority, power and dominion, and every title that can be given, not only in the present age but also in the one to come'.[26]

The Lord Jesus Christ's self-humbling, followed by exaltation in his Father's own good time, is the pattern for Christian discipleship. It is salutary to ask ourselves, 'With whom do I identify in this narrative? With Esther or with Haman?' And, remembering that the way up may be the way down, and vice versa, we do well to ask, 'Is God going to have to humble me? Or will he be able to lift me up? Upon which path are my feet?'

6.
God's perfect timing

Please read Esther 6

Casual conversations can sometimes be memorable. A number of years ago, while visiting a group of churches in Germany, I stayed a few days with a German family in a small town called Lüdenscheid. One day while we were out for a walk together, the father of the family remarked to me, 'God is never in a hurry!' I think he discerned that at that time, as a young man, I was all too easily impatient and that I wanted things to happen at once! I needed that counsel and have often reminded myself of it with profit. 'God is never in a hurry' or, to put it another way, God's timing is perfect.

Words of encouragement

Scripture illustrates Scripture. The narrative of this chapter, and, indeed, the whole book of Esther, points up truths taught elsewhere in the Bible, and especially in the books of Psalms and Proverbs. Take, for example, Psalm 37:5-7,32-33:

> Commit your way to the LORD;
>   trust in him and he will do this:
> he will make your righteousness shine like the dawn,
>   the justice of your cause like the noonday sun.

Be still before the LORD and wait patiently for him;
 do not fret when men succeed in their ways,
 when they carry out their wicked schemes...
The wicked lie in wait for the righteous,
 seeking their very lives;
but the LORD will not leave them in their power
 or let them be condemned when brought to trial.[1]

Vindication

The Scriptures assure faithful believers of their ultimate vindication by God. God promises not to overlook his people's cause.[2] Rather than attempting to champion our own rights, we are to recognize that the triumph of justice is God's proper work, and we are to look to him for it with confidence: 'Vindicate me, O God, and plead my cause,' the psalmist prays.[3] '"It is mine to avenge; I will repay," says the Lord.'[4] These and many other Scriptures confirm that evil will not finally prosper. They instruct us that the right attitudes to cultivate, when we are unjustly treated, are those of patience and believing submission to God's will and timing.

 This chapter illustrates some of these truths. We have arrived at the point where Esther has made her first approaches to the king. The survival of her people is at stake. Her first banquet has been held, and the second is to take place within hours.

An injustice discovered

The night following the first banquet found the king quite unable to sleep. To relieve his insomnia he might have called for music to be played, but instead — one of the book of Esther's

'coincidences' — he called for the record book, the chronicles of his reign, to be brought and read to him (6:1). Knowing from experience how sleep is encouraged as I listen to a
somewhat tedious BBC audio tape, I can appreciate how the
probably boring nature of the record book was calculated to
induce sleep for the king — however, not on this occasion, in
God's providence! This record of Xerxes' reign contained an
account of how Mordecai had denounced Bigthana and Teresh,
two of the king's eunuchs, who had been responsible for regu-
lating people's access to the king, for plotting to assassinate
Xerxes (2:21-22). How sadly contemporary it sounds!

The perfect timing of God's intervention may take our breath
away. On no other night was Mordecai in such danger. No
explanation is given for the king's sleeplessness — such as
worry, strong emotions, or physical discomfort. While Haman
no doubt slept well, with a false sense of security, King Xerxes
was awakened to his duty. It was wakefulness for which he
probably could not account. The sixteenth-century Puritan
Richard Sibbes aptly comments, 'Nothing so high, that is above
his providence, nothing so low, that is beneath it, nothing so
large, but it is bounded by it; nothing so confused, but God
can order it; nothing so bad, but he can draw good out of it;
nothing so wisely plotted, but God can disappoint it.' The king
'could not sleep, and thereupon calls for the chronicles, the
reading of which occasioned the Jews' delivery. God oft
disposeth little occasions to great purposes.'[5]

The royal archives contained an official list of those who
had acted on the king's behalf. It was a point of honour among
Persian kings to reward all benefactors. They are consistently
described by the historian Herodotus as having been generous
in rewarding loyal actions.[6] But for some reason Mordecai's
denunciation of the traitors had been overlooked. The king's
conscience began to work. **'What honour and recognition
has Mordecai received for this?'** the king asked. **'Nothing**

has been done for him,' the attendants answered him (6:3). Strangely, Mordecai's reward had been delayed.

The author of the book of Esther plainly expects discerning readers to see God's hand at work, both in the king's insomnia, and in the seeming accident of the point in the record from which the king's reader chose to read to him that night. God is never in a hurry. His timing and intervention are always exactly right.

A contrast

In passing we may draw a helpful contrast between King Xerxes and our King, our Lord and Saviour Jesus Christ. King Xerxes wanted to reward faithful subjects, but his human frailty meant that he made mistakes and overlooked things that had been done for him. How very different is our King! God has his own very special record book, as Malachi tells us: 'Those who feared the LORD talked with each other, and the Lord listened and heard. A scroll of remembrance was written in his presence concerning those who feared the LORD and honoured his name.'[7]

Matthew 25 reveals how surprised our Lord's faithful servants will be on the Day of Judgement at the perfect knowledge he has of all they have done in his name, both consciously and unconsciously: 'Then the King will say to those on his right, "Come, you who are blessed by my Father; take your inheritance, the kingdom prepared for you since the creation of the world. For I was hungry and you gave me something to eat, I was thirsty and you gave me something to drink, I was a stranger and you invited me in, I needed clothes and you clothed me, I was sick and you looked after me, I was in prison and you came to visit me." Then the righteous will answer him, "Lord, when did we see you hungry and feed you, or thirsty

and give you something to drink? When did we see you a
stranger and invite you in, or needing clothes and clothe you?
When did we see you sick or in prison and go to visit you?"
The King will reply, "I tell you the truth, whatever you did for
one of the least of these brothers of mine, you did for me." [8]

Hebrews 6:10 adds further confirmation: 'God is not unjust; he will not forget your work and the love you have shown
him as you have helped his people and continue to help them.'

An injustice rectified

When King Xerxes discovered the injustice done to Mordecai,
his response and action were immediate: **'Who is in the
court?'** It was plainly no accident that **'Haman had just en-
tered the outer court of the palace to speak to the king
about hanging Mordecai on the gallows he had erected
for him'** (6:4).

The king decided to ask Haman a question that must have
sounded like music to the latter's ears: **'What should be done
for the man the king delights to honour?'** (6:6). The verse
continues: **'Now Haman thought to himself…'** or, literally,
'Haman thought in his heart…' We think things in our hearts
that we may not express with our lips. Not surprisingly, Haman
thought to himself, **'Who is there that the king would rather
honour than me?'** With self as his god, he chose what would
satisfy his pride. And so he laid it on thick. **'He answered the
king, "For the man the king delights to honour, have them
bring a royal robe the king has worn and a horse the king
has ridden, one with a royal crest placed on its head. Then
let the robe and horse be entrusted to one of the king's
most noble princes. Let them robe the man the king delights to honour, and lead him on the horse through the
city streets, proclaiming before him, 'This is what is done**

for the man the king delights to honour!' "' (7-9) The bestowal of robes was common.[9] The Persian royal robe was thought by later Greek historians to possess magical power, and to confer a degree of royalty on its wearer. The royal 'crest', or crown, was an ornament for a king's horse (6:8). For Haman nothing less than everything associated with a king would suffice, together with the treatment that went with being a king (6:9).[10]

The king's response was immediate, but the sting was in the tail: **'Go at once... Get the robe and the horse and do just as you have suggested for Mordecai the Jew, who sits at the king's gate. Do not neglect anything you have recommended'** (6:10). Haman had no alternative but to obey (6:11). Perhaps we should try to imagine Haman's face! We can but guess what it cost him to do these things for his enemy. All the elements of the splendid picture conjured up by his fanciful imagination were bestowed upon Mordecai.

As for Mordecai, imagine his surprise! The rewards given to him were far beyond anything he could have imagined. His testimony was to be that of the writer of Psalm 124:

> We have escaped like a bird
>   out of the fowler's snare;
> the snare has been broken,
>   and we have escaped.
> Our help is in the name of the LORD,
>   the Maker of heaven and earth.[11]

His experience illustrates the wisdom which the Old Testament teaches: 'The prospect of the righteous is joy, but the hopes of the wicked come to nothing.'[12]

However, the major benefit was the perfect timing of the reward. Mordecai was known to be a Jew (6:10), and his loyal action, publicly rewarded in this way, proved that Jews were

no enemies to the king's person, contrary to Haman's evil suggestion (3:8). Furthermore, such unexpected honour must have
been a delightful indication to Mordecai that God was working on his people's behalf, in a manner which went far beyond
all he had asked or thought.

We cannot begin to imagine all that God may graciously
choose to do on behalf of his people. When it seems that God
is not active, he may be most at work. He may be most present
when he seems most hidden. His power is limitless, as are his
promises in our Lord Jesus Christ. By his Son's death for sinners he has achieved a perfect salvation for all who believe. As
part of that salvation in Christ, he freely gives his people all
they need.[13]

The irony of the situation in this chapter was that the instrument the king used for the bestowal of these benefits was
Mordecai's greatest enemy. Such is God's vindication of his
servants. Mordecai could have echoed Jeremiah's conviction:
'I know, O LORD, that a man's life is not his own; it is not for
man to direct his steps.'[14]

The information that **'Mordecai returned to the king's
gate'** (6:12) indicates something of his modesty and refusal to
allow events to go to his head. He returned to his duties as if
nothing had happened. More important than the robe with
which he had been dressed was the garment of humility.[15] Un-
like Haman he did not call all his friends together to enjoy
their congratulations and best wishes.

A warning given

Haman hurried home after his fulfilment of the king's instructions, to share the devastating news of his enemy's elevation.
His dejection could not be put into words. His wife, friends
and advisers could say nothing to comfort him. They now had

the conviction and settled belief that Haman was on the losing side (6:13). The Jews, God's people, were coming out on top. Everything now pointed that way for Haman, and so it turned out.

Verse 13 is a key verse and it expresses an essential message of the book of Esther: **'Since Mordecai, before whom your downfall has started, is of Jewish origin, you cannot stand against him — you will surely come to ruin!'** That assurance has been confirmed by human history.[16] Their advice now was completely different from what it had been before. Their observation confirmed that God was on the side of his people, and that their enemies could not prevail against them. While his friends and advisers **'were still talking with him, the king's eunuchs arrived and hurried Haman away to the banquet Esther had prepared'** (6:14). The verb translated 'hurried' indicates excitement or agitation.

There are many evidences of God's existence, and the continuing survival of the Jews as a distinct people, right up to this period of time in which we ourselves live, is one such. God's enemies conspire against his people in every age. Psalm 83 expresses their aim:

> With cunning they conspire against your people;
>   they plot against those you cherish.
> 'Come,' they say, 'let us destroy them as a nation,
>   that the name of Israel be remembered no more.'[17]

Frederick the Great once asked his personal physician, Zimmerman of Brugg in Aargau, 'Zimmerman, can you name me a single proof of the existence of God?' And Zimmerman replied, 'Your Majesty, the Jews!'

The church is similarly attacked by God's enemies as the people of God.[18] The continuance of the church of Jesus Christ, the new Israel, made up of redeemed Jews and Gentiles, is likewise a testimony to God's reality and power. A good example is the amazing growth of the church in China. At the close of the Cultural Revolution in 1978, for example, not one single official church was open. At the turn of the twenty-first century, there were over 13,000 as well as 35,000 registered meeting points and countless unregistered house churches.[19]

Satan's resources cannot prevail against the church of Jesus Christ.[20] With justified confidence Christians may ask, 'If God is for us, who can be against us?'[21]

A subject of relevance

There are lessons to apply to our own situations as we see God's work on behalf of the Jews in the days of Esther and Mordecai.

1. We should not fret over what seem to be God's 'delays'

We need to remember that God is always at work behind the scenes. It was so in Mordecai's case, and so it is in ours. We would be less than honest if we did not admit that delays are sometimes a problem to our faith,[22] but there are always wonderful purposes in them.[23] When the disciples were on the lake, there was a purpose in our Lord's not going to them until the fourth watch of the night,[24] as also in his delay in going to the grave of Lazarus.[25]

The poignant cry 'How long?' is often heard in the Psalms[26] where we also learn that, as Derek Kidner puts it, 'All God's delays are maturings, either of the time, as in Psalm 37, or the man, as in 119:67.'

2. We should rest in the sure knowledge of God's ultimate vindication

We do not have to look to the world for vindication, but to God. Whether or not people overlook what we have done is really a matter of indifference. God does not overlook us. He is able to reverse our fortunes.[27] A glorious time is fast approaching when God will right every wrong. Meanwhile, our Saviour, our ascended King, knows all we try to do in his name.

3. We should not fret over the opposition and difficulties God's people face in the world

Rather we should give ourselves to earnest prayer — as Esther, Mordecai and their fellow Jews did — and then give ourselves to God as instruments for the doing of his will, for the praise of his name.

Seldom, if ever, has God shown his power on behalf of his people without its having been preceded by some opposition against them. Without the difficulties, there would have been no triumphs. We do well to see all opposition and difficulties as a public platform or stage upon which God may display his power. And he will not disappoint us!

7.
This is the day

Please read Esther 7:1 – 8:8

Chapter 7 of the book of Esther illustrates the convictions of the writer of Psalm 73, who found himself perplexed by the prosperity of the wicked until he was given insight into what will happen to them in the end:

> When I tried to understand all this,
>   it was oppressive to me
> till I entered the sanctuary of God;
>   then I understood their final destiny.[1]

Every day is like a fresh blank sheet of paper given us by God, and we can never tell what wonderful surprises he may choose to write upon it. So much can happen in just a few hours. Our lives may proceed at an ordinary pace, with nothing of great importance appearing to happen. Then, suddenly, without warning, dramatic and amazing events may crowd into the space of a single day.

At this point in the narrative of Esther, prayer had been made for several days, seeking from God the deliverance of his people (4:15-17). On this particular day (7:2), which probably began like any other for the rest of the population, dramatic events took place, all demonstrating God's watchfulness. His people are described in the Old Testament as his vineyard, which he guards 'day and night so that no one may harm it'.[2] Or, changing the picture, he asks:

> Can a mother forget the baby at her breast
>   and have no compassion on the child she has borne?
> Though she may forget,
>   I will not forget you![3]

On any particular day remarkable developments and answers to our prayers may take place as God chooses to unfold his will, and demonstrate his care. On any day God may be at work in ways that we are not in a position to perceive. He weaves into the pattern of his will the actions of all his creatures, whether wise or foolish.

A day of revelation

While Haman's nearest relatives and advisers were still talking to him, the king's eunuchs arrived in a hurry to escort him to the banquet Esther had prepared (6:14). The word *'misteh'*, translated **'banquet'**, can be translated 'a banquet of wine', although it was used of a special meal prepared for honoured guests[4] or of wedding feasts.[5] The phrase translated, **'So the king and Haman went to dine with Queen Esther,'** literally says that they went to 'drink' with her. As wine is still often served at the beginning of special occasions, and more time may be spent in drinking than eating, so it was in Persia.

The time had come for Esther to make her special request, and the king did not allow her to forget it. By now he was probably intrigued to know what she wanted after all this build-up: **'Queen Esther, what is your petition? It will be given you...'** (7:2). The long wait before the request was made illustrates the truth that 'Through patience a ruler can be persuaded, and a gentle tongue can break a bone.'[6]

The plight of Esther's people compelled her to reveal her hitherto secret identity as a Jewess. Her reply to the king's request went straight to the point: **'If I have found favour with you, O king, and if it pleases your majesty, grant me my life — this is my petition. And spare my people — this is my request'** (7:3). The introduction to her petition is almost identical with the form of words she used in 5:8, when she issued the invitation to the second banquet. In the Hebrew, however, this time she adds the phrase **'in your eyes'**. This probably points to her intimacy with the king as his queen, and suggests that she was saying, in effect, 'If you really love me...' The king's addressing her as 'Queen Esther' (7:2), and his repetition of his promise to grant her even up to half of his kingdom, must have been a great encouragement to her as she freely admitted her Jewish birth and asserted her oneness with her people.

Esther's words provided a startling revelation, for both Haman and the king, as she brought out into the open the malicious plot to exterminate the Jews. **'For I and my people have been sold for destruction and slaughter and annihilation,'** she explained (7:4). No mention was made at this stage of Haman. Esther wanted to arouse the king's anger against the culprit before she was compelled to identify him as the king's favourite, to whom he had entrusted such authority. The word 'sold' may be an allusion to the monetary transaction between Haman and the king, or it may bear the sense of being 'delivered over to'.[7] The word translated **'distress'** occurs only here in the whole of the Old Testament, and it could be translated as 'injury' or 'damage', including financial harm. Esther indicated that what was happening was to the king's detriment, and clearly against his best interests.

Esther carefully stated the plot as it affected her and her people, without mentioning any names. By using the word **'I'** (7:4), and confessing her own part in the situation, she drew attention to the fact that her precarious position necessarily involved the king's honour as his queen. Anything that shamed her shamed the king. Notice how the narrative states that this compelled **'King Xerxes'** to ask **'Queen Esther'** the question: **'Who is he? Where is the man who dared to do such a thing?'** (7:5). Esther's answer was immediate: **'The adversary and enemy is this vile Haman'** (7:6). While evil schemes may be hidden, they cannot remain so. Although wicked works are planned in secret, the moment comes when God chooses to make them public.[8]

Days of revelation are in God's power. There was, for example, a day when God chose to reveal his amazing grace through the gift of his Son: 'When the time had fully come, God sent his Son, born of a woman, born under law, to redeem those under law, that we might receive the full rights of sons.'[9] On another unique day God revealed his Son's glory by raising him from the dead.[10]

There are days, too, when God brings to light men and women's secrets, whether to their confusion and shame, or their encouragement and gain. None may stop him, for, as the writer of Ecclesiastes says, 'God will bring every deed into judgement, including every hidden thing, whether it is good or evil.'[11]

A day of judgement

Haman quaked with fear (7:6), as he saw that the king was in a rage (7:7). Significantly, while Haman's fear is indicated, there is no evidence of regret or repentance.

The king left the banquet to go into the palace garden, for what reason we do not know. The words translated, **'The king had already decided his fate'** (7:7), are in the passive tense in the original. One version of the Bible translates these words as: 'He saw that evil was determined against him by the king.'[12]

This implies that the king was the device or instrument, but that the initiative came from a higher source. The king's dilemma was real. To deal with Haman was straightforward, apart from possible loss of face because he had given his royal approval to the scheme, but to rescind an irrevocable law was more difficult.

Haman, recognizing that the king was probably determined to ruin him, seized the opportunity to plead with Queen Esther to intervene on his behalf (7:7). The prophecy of his friends and advisers in 6:13 was being fulfilled. It is interesting that the same word is used in 6:13 of Haman's downfall as here in 7:8 of Haman's **'falling on the couch'** where Esther was reclining. The person intent on annihilating a Jew who refused to bow down to him found himself bowing down to a Jewess, pleading for mercy.

Persian etiquette demanded that a discreet distance be kept between any man and the king's wife. As the king returned to the room, he found Haman falling on the couch where Esther was reclining. If undecided before, the king was stirred to action now. He exclaimed, **'Will he even molest the queen while she is with me in the house?'** (7:8). 'Molest' has sexual overtones, but we should not read into this that Haman was literally intent on assaulting Esther, but rather that his action gave the king the opportunity to express his loathing of him. 'A king delights in a wise servant, but a shameful servant incurs his wrath.'[13] A veil was thrown over Haman's face (7:8) — the token of the death sentence. Both Greeks and Romans covered the heads of those condemned to death.

Harbona's observation that Haman had a seventy-five-foot (fifty cubits) high gallows by his house all ready for Mordecai had the effect of adding a second accusation against Haman, in that he was knowingly trying to kill one of the king's benefactors (7:9). The words of verse 10 — **'So they hanged Haman on the gallows he had prepared for Mordecai'** —

illustrate Old Testament wisdom.[14] Sin against others has the character of a boomerang.

Psalm 73 finds further illustration of its main arguments in the story of Haman and Mordecai. Many a Jew in Susa must have been perplexed as he walked past Haman's palatial home and witnessed his prosperity. Similarly puzzled by the prosperity of the wicked, the writer of the psalm went into God's sanctuary. There God gave him understanding to appreciate what is before men and women who appear to thrive on wickedness:

> Surely you place them on slippery ground;
>> you cast them down to ruin.
> How suddenly are they destroyed,
>> completely swept away by terrors!
> As a dream when one awakes,
>> so when you arise, O LORD,
>> you will despise them as fantasies.[15]

In a moral universe all bills must be paid. The Sovereign LORD is the righteous judge. 'He catches the wise in their craftiness, and the schemes of the wily are swept away.'[16] 'Judgement without mercy will be shown to anyone who has not been merciful.'[17] 'Therefore judge nothing before the appointed time,' instructs Paul; 'wait till the Lord comes. He will bring to light what is hidden in darkness and will expose the motives of men's hearts. At that time each will receive his praise from God.'[18] We may often be in danger of underestimating or failing to declare this part of God's counsel.[19]

A day of rewards

Since Haman was a traitor, his entire estate automatically reverted to the crown (8:1). As the book of Proverbs teaches,

'A good man leaves an inheritance for his children's children, but a sinner's wealth is stored up for the righteous.'[20] The king gave the estate to Esther as some tangible compensation for her suffering. Esther, in turn, appointed Mordecai over it, maintaining her legal possession of it, but with Mordecai as her agent. The king then proceeded to appoint Mordecai to office in place of Haman (8:2).

It was undeniably a day of rewards. Haman's reward was the gallows he had so carefully and maliciously set apart for Mordecai, and Mordecai was rewarded with the possessions Haman had reserved for himself. Haman found it to be as our Lord Jesus declared: 'For in the same way as you judge others, you will be judged, and with the measure you use, it will be measured to you.'[21]

While the coming Judgement Day is certain, aspects of God's judgement may sometimes be seen to be working themselves out in the present. What, however, is not worked out in the present will unfailingly be worked out in the future. As Richard Sibbes (1577-1633) put it, 'There will be a resurrection of credits as well as of bodies.' The Lord Jesus will give to believers precisely what their works deserve.[22] The day of final judgement will be a day of rewards.

A day for action

The enemy may have been defeated, but his schemes still needed to be frustrated. Haman's ruin had been achieved, but the plan he had devised still remained in operation. We have to say the same of our enemy Satan. His defeat was achieved at Calvary, but his schemes still need to be frustrated in this period before his final end.

Realizing the urgency of the situation, Esther pleaded with the king. No indication is given of the timing of Esther's pleading recorded in 8:3, but it does not seem to have been a fresh audience with the king. She prostrated herself before him as she acted as intercessor for her people. In 4:8 Mordecai had instructed her to 'beg for mercy and plead' with the king for her people, and this she now did. She matched words with actions as she fell at his feet, weeping. She could not, and would not, separate herself from her people.[23] Her speech was very much in the spirit of Paul's concern for his Jewish kith and kin: 'I speak the truth in Christ — I am not lying, my conscience confirms it in the Holy Spirit — I have great sorrow and unceasing anguish in my heart. For I could wish that I myself were cursed and cut off from Christ for the sake of my brothers, those of my own race.'[24] **'She begged him to put an end to the evil plan of Haman the Agagite'** (8:3-6), no doubt recognizing the dilemma this presented to the king because of the nature of Persian law, which could not be repealed (1:19).

Esther's action resulted in the king's giving authority to Esther and Mordecai to do whatever they could to counter the earlier decree. **'King Xerxes replied to Queen Esther and to Mordecai the Jew, "Because Haman attacked the Jews, I have given his estate to Esther, and they have hanged him on the gallows. Now write another decree in the king's name on behalf of the Jews as seems best to you, and seal it with the king's signet ring — for no document written in the king's name and sealed with his ring can be revoked"'** (8:7-8). He handed over to them the whole responsibility for the reversal of Haman's evil plans. In verse 8 the king says in effect, 'I have done my part; it is now up to you to do yours.' It is similar to Pilate's statement: 'What I have written, I have written.'[25] The king's words, 'No document written in the king's name and sealed with his ring can be revoked,' were typical of the proud arrogance of the Persian kings. Significantly, Mordecai is identified once more as 'the Jew', and Esther as 'Queen Esther' (8:7). 'The Jew' has become Mordecai's fixed title.[26]

'This is the day'

This whole passage prompts a salutary question. When God is
at work for us, who may guess what any day may bring forth?
Of every day we may say, 'This is the day the LORD has made;
let us rejoice and be glad in it,' and we may go on, as in the
next verse of the psalm, and say, 'O LORD, save us; O LORD,
grant us success.'[27]

Perhaps today may be *a day of revelation*. There may be
those to whom God would have us reveal our identity as believers, by the kind of life we live and the words we speak.
There may be evil schemes that God is going to bring out into
the open today. Let us so live that we may have nothing secret
of which to be ashamed.

Perhaps today may be *a day of judgement*. It may be that
sins against others are going to boomerang today on those
responsible. Let us so live that we have only good things that
can rebound on us.

Perhaps today may be *a day of rewards*. Not all of God's
rewards are left until the final Day of Judgement. The Lord
Jesus promised, 'No one who has left home or brothers or
sisters or mother or father or children or fields for me and the
gospel will fail to receive a hundred times as much in this
present age ... and in the age to come, eternal life.'[28] Let us
strive to live in glad obedience to the Lord Jesus so that we
deserve his reward — in so far as it is possible for unprofitable
servants to do so.

And perhaps today may be *a day for action*. There may be
key initiatives or actions we are to take today for the good of
others, and for God's praise. During the Methodist Conference in the year in which he was president, Dr Sangster distributed a letter to those present at the Sunday morning service in which he stressed the importance of action, and in which
he shared a most helpful practice. He wrote, 'For years it has

been my practice at the time of morning prayer to have a part of my notebook headed "Action". Here I have been glad to put anything which came to me in the quietness as something God wanted me to do ... and this, at the earliest opportunity, I have done. It introduced a little method into my Methodism and saved me from indulging in feelings which never became facts!'

Today is *a day never to be repeated*. Let us live it for God!

8.
Tables turned!

Please read Esther 8:9 – 9:15

King Xerxes' dilemma was acute. The edict he had made, at Haman's instigation, could not be revoked. This was a principle laid down in the laws of Persia and Media (1:19). He recognized nevertheless that there were ways and means of achieving his purpose. He gave Esther and Mordecai a free hand to draw up another edict that would somehow or other render the first one harmless to the Jews (8:8).

'At once the royal secretaries were summoned — on the twenty-third day of the third month, the month of Sivan. They wrote out all Mordecai's orders to the Jews, and to the satraps, governors and nobles of the 127 provinces stretching from India to Cush. These orders were written in the script of each province and the language of each people and also to the Jews in their own script and language' (8:9).¹ The day appointed was **'the thirteenth day of the twelfth month, the month of Adar'** (8:12). Mordecai had authority to write **'in the name of King Xerxes'**, so that it was plain that the edict was not his, but carried royal authority. It was sent **'by mounted couriers, who rode fast horses especially bred for the king'** (8:10), the best express postal system available.

This new edict allowed Jews in every city to gather together to protect themselves. They were given authority to

'destroy, kill and annihilate any armed force of any nationality or province that might attack them and their women
and children' (8:11). Initially this may seem rather blood-
thirsty and revengeful. However, the last words of verse 11 in
Hebrew — 'to plunder the property of their enemies' —
come from Haman's original edict against the Jews (see 3:13).
The Jews were given permission to retaliate in the manner
planned by Haman against them. Their goal was simply to re-
pulse their attackers. Anything less would have resulted in their
annihilation. While they were given 'the right' to plunder the
property of their enemies, they were not obliged to do so. Just
one day was appointed for these things to take place — the
same day as Haman had fixed for the Jews' destruction, the
thirteenth day of the twelfth month, the month of Adar (8:12;
cf. 3:7).

The right to assemble themselves together (8:11) was important for the successful counteraction of the plot against
them. If Jews had not been permitted to gather until the intended day of slaughter, preventative action would have been
impossible. The new edict was a life-saving decree, and messengers rode out with appropriate haste (8:14), so that all in
danger should know of the way of escape. Jews were given
permission to defend themselves — that was the essence of
the message. Distances of up to two thousand miles were involved, so speed was essential.

The transformation God's deliverance brings

The deliverance God was providing for his people became
tangible to them as they saw Mordecai coming out from the
king's presence wearing a princely gown of blue and white,
with a large golden crown and a cloak of fine linen and purple
(8:15). If Mordecai clothed in sackcloth symbolized the Jews

in trouble, Mordecai dressed in purple symbolized the Jews in triumph. His clothes were an indication of the amazing status the king now gave him. Chapter 1 includes purple as being among the rich and luxurious royal accessories of Xerxes' feast (1:6), a sign of honour and royalty.

Mordecai was not acting for himself alone, but was his people's representative. Because he had appeared successfully in the king's presence on their behalf, Jews everywhere were to be delivered.

'And the city of Susa held a joyous celebration' (8:15). In chapter 3 Haman's edict had brought grief to the city, but now Mordecai's exaltation prompted joy. This again indicates that Haman's hostility to the Jews was not representative of the Persian population as a whole, since the latter appear not only to have been tolerant of the Jews, but to have held them in high esteem. Old Testament wisdom is again confirmed:

When the righteous prosper, the city rejoices,
　when the wicked perish, there are shouts of joy.
Through the blessing of the upright a city is exalted,
　but by the mouth of the wicked it is destroyed.[2]

Throughout the city of Susa, and **'in every province and in every city'** the joyful celebrations of the Jewish people could be heard (8:17). There was joy and gladness, feasting and holidaymaking everywhere among the Jews as the message reached them.

Some translations of verse 16 (e.g. the Authorized Version and the Revised Standard Version) express the thought that the Jews had **'light and gladness and joy and honour'**. Mordecai's victory symbolized and proclaimed the victory and its benefits that belonged to all Jews. Light is an Old Testament symbol for prosperity and well-being.[3] Psalm 27 begins:

> The LORD is my light and my salvation —
>> whom shall I fear?
> The LORD is the stronghold of my life —
>> of whom shall I be afraid?[4]

After the darkness of despair that had descended upon them, the Jews were now aware of light. The sun had broken through their storm-filled clouds, and everything was gloriously transformed.

The Jews experienced gladness. They were able to echo the last words of David:

> The God of Israel spoke,
>> the Rock of Israel said to me:
> 'When one rules over men in righteousness,
>> when he rules in the fear of God,
> he is like the light of morning at sunrise
>> on a cloudless morning,
> like the brightness after rain
>> that brings the grass from the earth.[5]

The Jews wanted to shout and sing. In place of sorrow, they had joy, the joy of faith and hope, since their deliverance was not yet complete. Instead of insults and the threat of injury, they had honour. The contrast between their position, as they put their faith in God, and Haman's position, who put his trust in the casting of lots, was complete. The tables had been completely turned.

'Many people of other nationalities became Jews because fear of the Jews had seized them' (8:17). Promises of God in Scripture were fulfilled. 'This is what the LORD Almighty says: "Many peoples and the inhabitants of many cities will yet come, and the inhabitants of one city will go to another and say, 'Let us go at once to entreat the LORD and seek the LORD

Almighty. I myself am going.' And many peoples and powerful nations will come to Jerusalem to seek the LORD Almighty
and to entreat him."'[6] The reference in 9:27 to those who
joined them suggests that there were genuine converts among
the people who were seen to adopt the faith of the Jews, and
that their profession was not just a sham. While fear may have
been a predominant motive, it was not an altogether unworthy
reason for their action. As Isaiah prophesied, 'The LORD will
have compassion on Jacob... Aliens will join them and unite
with the house of Jacob.'[7]

Glorious parallels in our experience

While God's delivering grace has varied applications, God's
people in every period of history can identify with one another
in their experience of it. Our Saviour is Jesus Christ, the Son
of God. When he died and rose again, it was for us. As our
Saviour he ascended into heaven and sat down in the place of
honour at the right hand of God, and again he did so on our
behalf. As the Jews were identified with Mordecai, so we are
identified in a far more wonderful way with our Lord Jesus
Christ. His triumph is our triumph. He promises us victory
over all our enemies.

   As the people rejoiced when they saw Mordecai robed and
crowned, so we rejoice in our Saviour and his position: 'We
see Jesus, who was made a little lower than the angels, now
crowned with glory and honour.'[8] We recall our Saviour's
words from the cross, 'It is finished!' and his triumphant rising again from the dead, and we know that salvation has been
accomplished, and is freely available to all who believe. His
sitting down at the Father's right hand is an added confirmation of his completed work.

Wherever the messengers of the King of kings go, the acceptance of this deliverance brings similar benefits to those which the Jews experienced at their deliverance from Haman's evil plans.

In our Lord Jesus Christ we have light, for he is the light of the world. He chases away the darkness of sin and Satan from our lives. He gives us light to understand God's truth. He throws light upon our path throughout life. He gives spiritual prosperity. We find unspeakable gladness in him, for he becomes everything to us. We know a joy in him that has the touch of heaven about it.[9] The honour God bestows upon us in our Lord Jesus Christ is breathtaking: 'Now we are children of God, and what we will be has not yet been made known. But we know that when he appears, we shall be like him, for we shall see him as he is.'[10]

Christian rejoicing ought to more than match the rejoicing of Jews in Persia in the fifth century B.C. We ought to feel a similar urgent constraint to send out messengers to all who have not yet heard the gospel's message, and we should do so with haste (cf. 8:14). Tragically there are men and women who still live their lives looking to the stars and their horoscopes rather than to the living God and trusting in the message of his salvation.

The retribution that is sadly necessary in a fallen world

On the very day when the enemies of the Jews had hoped to get mastery over them, the Jews gained the mastery over their foes (9:1). The Jews stood ready to lay hands on any who sought to harm any of their number (9:2). Furthermore, **'All the nobles of the provinces, the satraps, the governors and the king's administrators helped the Jews, because fear of Mordecai had seized them'** (9:3). 'Fear of Mordecai' has been compared to 'the Fear of Isaac' in Genesis 31:42, where it is a way of speaking of God. If the comparison is correct, then a further reference to God is found here in the book of Esther in addition to those alluded to in the introduction. The Jews also struck down all their known enemies (9:5): five hundred were destroyed initially in Susa, and Haman's ten sons were also killed (6-12).

Massacre and bloodshed are abuses about which Christians can never be happy. We live in a harsh and sinful world, however, where only the well-timed exercise of judgement places a restraint upon the ever-threatening escalation of sin. The Jews had not initiated the hostility. Few, if any, of them had originally chosen to live in the Persian Empire. If we find ourselves inclined to condemn the Jews for the slaughter of their known enemies, we should remember the complete and utter annihilation with which they had been threatened.

The vengeance exercised by the Jews was in self-defence. Even after the deliverance Esther had been instrumental in bringing about, their lives were not safe all the time Haman's associates and family remained alive. They were acting in self-defence. They were not the aggressors.

While it is only on the great Day of Judgement that God's judgement will be exercised in its entirety, he chooses to exercise it now in some measure where restraint is urgent in order to prevent the uncontrollable escalation of violence, and where evil actions hinder his gracious purposes in human lives.

The display of the bodies of Haman's sons after their execution was probably intended as a further dishonour to his name, and a warning to any other enemies of the Jews (9:6-10,13,14). Their enemies needed to have terror struck into their minds and hearts lest they perpetuated their animosity against the Jews.[11]

Those who deny the necessity for drastic examples of judgement upon unrighteousness fail to grapple with the harsh realities of life in a world that is in rebellion against God. While the retribution was harsh, it was just. Because of the hardness of men and women's hearts, severe acts of judgement are inevitable in human history.

The Lord Jesus loved the people of Jerusalem, and wept over them.[12] But, for the most part, they rejected him and the message of salvation he proclaimed to them. There is no doubt that the fall and destruction of Jerusalem in A.D. 70 were part of the outworking of God's just judgement. In any unjust situation we do not know whether God will delay his judgement or not, but we may be sure that he will exercise it at the appropriate time.

No plunder

Three times in the narrative an indication is given of the restraint that ought to be placed on natural acquisitiveness. Emphasis is placed upon the Jews' refusal to plunder, although they had official permission to take what they wished. The king's edict had specifically authorized them to plunder their enemies' possessions (8:11). But as verses 10, 15 and 16 declare, **'They did not lay their hands on the plunder.'** Such strength of will cannot have been easy. We are all naturally acquisitive. Most of us appreciate getting something for nothing. The Jews might have argued that if they did not take the plunder themselves others would. But they did not succumb to the temptation.

Survival, not plunder, was what they were fighting for. By their refusal to gather booty, they gave witness to the God whom they served. They showed by their behaviour his justice and holiness. If they had taken plunder, people could have suggested that the reason why the Jews slaughtered their enemies was to gain their possessions. But no such criticism was possible.

Perhaps, too, they had wisely adopted Abraham's philosophy about the acquisition of wealth. Abraham rescued his nephew Lot, and the King of Sodom offered Abraham the plunder that legitimately went with his victory. 'But Abram said to the king of Sodom, "I have raised my hand to the LORD, God Most High, Creator of heaven and earth, and have taken an oath that I will accept nothing belonging to you, not even a thread or the thong of a sandal, so that you will never be able to say, 'I made Abram rich.'"'[13] The Jews' ancestors in the time of Saul had foolishly disobeyed God by being more concerned to plunder the Amalekites than to obey God;[14] now this generation wisely refrained from plunder when they had every reason and right to take their enemies' possessions.

By this careful avoidance of greed the Jews showed that their principal joy and cause for celebration was God's deliverance (8:16-17). Possessions are a good gift from God, and none of us would find life easy without many of them. But they can constitute a considerable snare. They can become a major preoccupation, and the root of covetousness that is idolatry.[15] They can choke the effectiveness of God's Word in our lives.[16]

The key factor is whether we deliberately aim at adding to our possessions or whether we allow God to add them to us. If we make the pursuit of possessions our goal, they are more than likely to become too important and dangerous. If, however, we put first the kingdom of God, and doing what is right, then he will add to us all that we need — and often far more. Our possessions will then be a blessing, and not a snare. Where our treasure is, there our hearts will be too. If our hearts are genuinely with our Lord Jesus Christ, then our treasures will be in heaven, where he is.[17]

9.
Lest we forget

Please read Esther 9:16 – 10:3

To celebrate deliverance is natural and usual. If lessons are to be learned from it, it is appropriate to perpetuate its remembrance. While history records dramatic reversals of the fortunes of God's people, few can rival what took place at the time when Esther and Mordecai were the chief characters.

Every year Jews celebrate this deliverance in the festival of Purim. It is in the spring, a month before Passover. For Jews, and especially Jewish children, it is very much a fun day, when they often dress up as the different characters in the story of Esther. Every time Haman's name is mentioned, hissing and booing, the stamping of feet and the waving of rattles drown it, whereas every mention of Mordecai is greeted with cheering. Pastries called 'Haman's ears' and 'pockets' are eaten. Children take gifts of food to the elderly. The day is spent in what is altogether a party atmosphere. But the celebration is not confined to children. In the undergraduate newspaper at Cambridge the following diary announcement appeared:

CAMBRIDGE UNIVERSITY JEWISH SOCIETY: SIDNEY CAMPAIGN AGAINST RACISM: Persian Fancy Dress Party to celebrate the Purim Festival: Knox-Shaw Room. Sidney: 8.30 p.m.

The intention of the festival

One of the principal purposes of the book of Esther is to explain how this non-Mosaic festival of Purim became part of the Jewish calendar.

The word *'pur'* is not a Hebrew word and is almost certainly Assyrian, meaning 'lot', referring to Haman's casting of lots to find a lucky day to attack the Jews (3:7; 9:24,26). The term *'puru'*, meaning 'lot', has been discovered in Assyrian inscriptions.

The Jews called the Feast 'Purim' to remind them of the lot that had been cast for their destruction but which led instead to their deliverance. They called it in effect 'lottery day', for it was the day on which the predictions of the lot were falsified, and threatened misfortune was turned into good fortune.

On the thirteenth day of Adar they killed their opponents (9:16-17). On the fourteenth day they rested and made it a day of feasting, gladness, holidaymaking and an occasion for exchanging presents (9:17-19).

The institution of the festival

The official institution of the Purim Festival appears to rest upon three actions.

1. Mordecai sent letters to all the Jews throughout the provinces of the kingdom (9:20-22)

He instructed them to celebrate the fourteenth and fifteenth days of the month of Adar every year as the days on which **'the Jews got relief from their enemies'**. He encouraged them to observe these dates as days of festivity and gladness when they were to exchange presents of food with one another and make gifts to the poor.

When, later, Nehemiah called the Jewish people to celebrate another important occasion in their history, he said, 'Go and enjoy choice food and sweet drinks, and send some to those who have nothing prepared. This day is sacred to our Lord. Do not grieve, for the joy of the LORD is your strength.'[1] His concern was similarly for those who might have little or nothing with which to celebrate.

2. The Jews carefully adopted Mordecai's directions (9:23,27-28)

They undertook to continue these practices in the future. They vowed and committed themselves and their descendants — and all who should join them — to celebrate on these days. They determined that the two days of Purim should never be put aside among the Jews. According to Josephus, the two days of official observance of Purim were accepted by the Jews, and by the time of the codification of Jewish oral law in the Mishnah (around A.D. 200) they had become legalized in the Jewish calendar.

3. Esther and Mordecai's confirmatory letter served to settle its institution (9:29-31)

So, too, did Mordecai's continued eminence (10:1-3). Fasting here (9:31) was clearly associated with religious faith, as it was earlier (4:16), and 'lamentation' with prayer. The basic meaning of the word 'lamentation' is to cry for help in time of distress. It is used almost exclusively of a cry from a disturbed heart, in need of some kind of help. Most frequently, the cry is directed to God.[2]

Esther's decree further established this observance of Purim, and it was recorded in writing (9:32). The word **'decree'** is *'ma'amar'*, the same term used when Xerxes commanded

Vashti to appear before him (1:15), and when Mordecai commanded Esther to keep her Jewish identity a secret (2:20). Its use underlines her royal status and new prominence.

The opening verse of chapter 10 indicates that the king's financial resources benefited from the Jews' success over their enemies. Mordecai's situation was like that of Joseph when Pharaoh told him centuries earlier, 'You shall be in charge of my palace, and all my people are to submit to your orders. Only with respect to the throne will I be greater than you.'[3] Daniel was elevated to a similar position in the court of Belshazzar.[4]

'Mordecai the Jew was second in rank to King Xerxes, pre-eminent among the Jews, and held in high esteem by his many fellow Jews, because he worked for the good of his people and spoke up for the welfare of all the Jews' (10:3). He is an example of what we read of in Galatians 6:10: 'As we have opportunity, let us do good to all people, especially to those who belong to the family of believers.' Quakers have a saying: 'Do all the good you can, and to all the people you can, in all the ways you can.'

Remembrance

An important lesson of this whole episode is that God's deliverance of his people is to be deliberately and carefully remembered. Mordecai's concern was that those who had passed through these harrowing experiences should never forget what God had done for them (9:20-23), and that they should ensure that their descendants also commemorated the deliverance, because their existence and preservation also flowed from it.

One of the central features of the Christian life — the most important — is the remembrance of God's delivering grace, of his gracious gift of salvation through the death of our

Saviour. It is impossible to live as we ought without recognizing its priority. Central to God's deliverance of his people is the atoning death of his Son. The cross is both simple and profound: simple in that a child may understand why the Lord Jesus died, and profound because none who are saved by it can ever plumb its depths.

The amazing knowledge that our Saviour shed his blood to redeem us is to influence every part of our daily life. It humbles us as we realize how great our sins are, so that our Saviour had to die for us, and that there is no other way by which we may be reconciled to God. It lifts us up as we appreciate how much God must love us, and how completely and finally our Saviour dealt with all our sins.

The Lord's Supper

To keep the cross and its significance central we also have a feast. It is not a feast of human appointment, but appointed by our Saviour himself. The Lord Jesus appointed what we know as 'the Lord's Supper' to keep his death for us central in our thinking, so that, as individuals and as members of his body, we may live always taking into account what he has achieved for us. He set up this meal, not that we should meet on an annual basis, and not even on a weekly or daily basis, but as often as we can do so together.

The Lord's Day

One of the principal purposes of the Lord's Supper, or communion service, like the Feast of Purim, is remembrance. As the Lord Jesus Christ took both the bread and the wine, he said, 'Do this in remembrance of me.'[5] While the Lord's Supper may be celebrated on any day of the week, there is particular appropriateness about its observance on a Sunday.[6]

The change from the seventh to the first day of the week arose from our Lord Jesus' resurrection on that day, and the recognition that it is a special day for Christians to meet to worship and seek God together.[7] Early Christians understood that their observance of the fourth commandment did not demand a literal observance of Saturday as the Sabbath but rather keeping one day in seven to recall their dependence upon God as their Creator and Redeemer, as his 'exodus' people had done under the old covenant.[8]

What the Festival of Purim can teach us

The Festival of Purim has four features that are applicable and appropriate to our celebration of the Lord's Supper and the Lord's Day: rest, feasting, gladness and the exercise of generosity (9:17-19,22).

Rest

Both the Lord's Supper and the Lord's Day provide a particular kind of rest. In effect, our Saviour says, 'Come with me by yourselves to a quiet place and get some rest.'[9] If there is no rest, no stopping, there can be no proper remembrance or meditation upon what is remembered. Without meditation, there can be no real worship.

Feasting

Both the Lord's Supper and the Lord's Day are occasions for a special kind of feasting. The early Christians gave themselves to the apostles' doctrine and fellowship, and to the breaking of bread and prayers.[10] Breaking bread in their homes, they partook of their food with glad and generous hearts.[11]

They feasted upon God's revelation in that they sat under the instruction of God's Word as the apostles taught them. They feasted upon fellowship in the Lord Jesus Christ as they recognized their common relationship to him and to one another. They feasted spiritually at the Lord's Supper as they meditated upon our Saviour's saving work and their union with him. They feasted as they shared in one another's hospitality, remembering that they were now one body and one family.

Sadly, it is possible not to give the Lord's Supper and the Lord's Day the place they ought to have. We need to remind ourselves that it is the Lord Jesus himself who invites us to his table. Every time it is spread, he is the host, and we are his invited guests. To appreciate this truth will mean that we always take seriously the invitation to share in his Supper and respond whenever we can.

The Lord's Day is similarly his day. Our most important duty, therefore, is to use it in those ways we know will please him. The secularization of society makes the keeping of Sunday special increasingly difficult. That makes all the more important our valuing of it, and the testimony we give to our faith by making it a special day each week. Rather than a day for the supermarket like any other, it is to be seen as the 'supermarket' day for our souls, when we obtain our spiritual supplies for the new week ahead. Rather than a negative motivation, as some might suggest, the idea of keeping Sunday is entirely positive because it gives us a complete break and a day to think about the one who counts most in our life, and to regain a right perspective on the cares of life. It is the best antidote to worldliness.

Gladness

Both the Lord's Supper and the Lord's Day are occasions of gladness. While the Lord's Supper commemorates the sad night on which our Lord was betrayed, and the awesome truth that he bore God's wrath against our sins, it also commemorates his love for us — and we rejoice!

Furthermore, as the Lord's Day itself reminds us, we worship and love a risen Saviour, who is unchanging and who promises to be with us always. The Lord's Day is the day of days in the week to his people. Our praise and prayers should express our gladness.

Generosity

Both the Lord's Supper and the Lord's Day are opportunities for the expression of generosity. At the Lord's Supper it has been traditional in many churches to take up a 'fellowship offering' to be used for the relief and help of Christians in financial or material need. On the Lord's Day we may bring our monetary gifts as part of our worship of him and our fellowship together. In addition, on the Lord's Day most of us have more leisure to exercise generous hospitality, not only to those who are in a position to return it, but also especially to those who are not.

The danger of forgetfulness

Esther and Mordecai were mindful of the dangers of forgetfulness. When perils are past, feelings of thankfulness all too often evaporate. The Israelites, for example, soon forgot the harsh realities of their slavery in Egypt, and even drew an idealized picture of life there when times became difficult in the wilderness period.[12]

Esther and Mordecai's joint concern was that neither they nor their fellow Jews should ever forget God's mercy. There was always the danger that over the years the feast might become a somewhat meaningless ritual. But all the time the feast was observed, there was a greater likelihood that people would remember the events that it commemorated.

Over the Feast of Purim, then, we can write the one word, 'Remember'. Over the Lord's Supper and the Lord's Day we can write the same. Our proneness to forget demands that we use helps that stimulate our memory. The Jewish Passover Feast is also essentially a commemorative feast — a stimulus to memory.[13] Psalms urge God's people to 'forget not all his benefits'.[14] Such commemorations and exhortations are necessary and we should not find them irksome if we know that they are for our safety.[15] As we help our memories to focus upon our Lord and Saviour, we find the secret of spiritual strength and perseverance. To remember Jesus Christ is to fan the flames of our faith into a fire that both warms and empowers.

The remembrance of our indebtedness to the Lord Jesus should not be an annual event but a daily practice. Writing to the Corinthians, Paul likens the Christian life to a continuous festival.[16] Every day I should remind myself that I am not my own because I have been bought with a price. As Martin Luther put it, 'I feel as if Jesus had died only yesterday.' Catching sight off the coast of Greece of a ruin topped by a cross outlined against the sky, David Adeney, a missionary with the Overseas Missionary Fellowship and founder of the Discipleship Training Centre in Singapore, was profoundly moved at the thought that 'The Cross is the reason for everything I'm doing.'[17]

References

It was necessary to decide whether to put references in the text of the commentary or as an appendix. Since there are so many, it seems helpful to separate them from the commentary so that it may be read more readily, as any other book, but, at the same time, for those who want to study the book of Esther in a more detailed fashion, perhaps in personal or group Bible study, or with a view to teaching and preaching, to include them.

While few will want to pursue the references to sources such as Herodotus and Josephus, they have been included even if only to remind us how firmly anchored the book is in history.

Introduction
1. Gen. 50:20.
2. See Lev. 26; Deut. 28; 29.
3. Ezra 2; 3:2,8; 4:1-3.
4. See 1 Peter 5:13; Rev. 17:5-6,9,15,18; 18:2-3,9.
5. See Ezra 6:15; Esth. 3:7.
6. Esth. 3:5; 5:9,10,11,14; 6:12; 7:6.
7. Esth. 3:6; 6:6; 7:7.
8. 1 Cor. 1:27.
9. Josephus, *Antiquities of the Jews,* 11:6:1.
10. Esth. 1:1,13-14; 4:11; 8:8; 10:2.
11. Josephus, *Contr. Apionem,* i. 8.
12. The Septuagint gets its name from the Greek word for 'seventy', because of the number of scholars who translated it. It is often referred to by means of the symbol LXX, which is 70 in Roman numerals.
13. Luke 24:25-27.
14. Rom. 11:33-36.
15. Matt. 2:16.

16. John 4:22.
17. Gen. 3:15.
18. John 1:14,17.

Chapter 1 — Majesty, alcohol and example

1. Isa. 40:14; Rom. 11:33; Rev. 21:6.
2. He was the fourth king in the Archaemenian period of Persian history (550 – 331 B.C.). Before his accession to the throne, Darius I had three sons by one wife, and after his accession he had four more by Atossa. The eldest of the first three was Artabazanes. Xerxes was the eldest of the four by Atossa and he succeeded to the throne because he was born after his father's accession.

The Greek historian Herodotus gives a detailed history of Xerxes, and Josephus, the Jewish historian, adds his contribution. Herodotus reckoned that Xerxes would have followed his father anyway because of the influence of his mother. His position has been assessed as follows: 'He had round him his father's captains; he had immense resources in gold and in manpower, and he failed; and at every point the chief source of Persian weakness seems to have been the fact that the man, who had at last to decide everything, was unequal to the task' (T. R. Glover, *The Ancient World*, Pelican Books, 1948, p.99).
3. Herodotus, *History,* VII, 187.
4. It continues: 'Thus speaks King Xerxes: These are the countries — in addition to Persia — of which I am king under the "shadow" of Ahuramazda, over which I hold sway, which are bringing their tribute to me — whatever is commanded them by me, that they do, and they abide by my law[s]: Media, Elam, Arachosia, Urartu, Drangiana, Parthia, [H]aria, Bactria, Sogdia, Chorasmia, Babylonia, Assyria, Sattagydia, Sardis, Egypt *(Misir)*, the Ionians who live on the salty sea and [those] who live beyond ... the salty sea, Maka, Arabia, Gandara, India, Cappadocia, Da'an, the Amyrgian Cimmerians ... [wearing] pointed caps, the Skudra, the Akupsih, Libya, Banneshu [Carians and] Kush' (J. B. Pritchard, *Ancient Near Eastern Texts* (1955), pp.316-17).
5. Herodotus, *History,* III, 97; VII 9, 65, 69f.
6. Herodotus, *History,* VII, 8.
7. Herodotus, *The Histories*, Penguin Classics, 1972, pp.443-5, 463-4.
8. Prov. 24:6.
9. Cf. Eccles. 10:16-17; Isa. 5:11.
10. Cf. Eccles. 8:4.
11. Rom. 13:1.
12. Rom. 13:2.
13. Rev. 17:14.
14. Ps. 2:6,8-9; 110:1-2; Isa. 9:6-7; Dan. 7:14.
15. John 19:19,20.
16. Phil. 2:9.
17. Rom. 14:9.
18. Rev. 1:5.
19. Rev. 17:14; 19:16.
20. Phil. 2:9-11.
21. Rev. 5:6.
22. Isa. 6:1; cf. John 12:41.

23. Matt. 26:29.
24. Eph. 3:8.
25. Rom. 9:23; Eph. 3:16.
26. Eph. 1:7; 2:7.
27. Matt. 28:18.
28. Rev. 5:13; 12:10.
29. John 14:19.
30. 2 Tim. 2:12.
31. Cf. 1 Sam. 25:36.
32. Herodotus, *History,* VII: 61.
33. J. S. Wright, 'The Historicity of the Book of Esther,' in *New Perspectives on the Old Testament*, ed. J. Barton Payne (Waco: Word, 1970), pp.40-41.
34. Herodotus, *The Histories*, p.105.
35. Eunuchs, castrated human males, were employed as guards and servants in harems or other women's quarters, and as chamberlains to kings. They were considered the most suitable guards for the many wives or concubines a ruler might have in his palace. Their confidential position often enabled them to exercise an important influence over their masters and even to gain positions of great trust and power. Most underwent castration as a condition of their employment, though others were castrated as punishment, or after poor parents had sold them. When we find the words meaning an 'official' or 'court officer' in the Old Testament it is often a word implying castration, i.e. eunuchs.
36. See, e.g., 2:2,3,7.
37. Josephus, *Antiquities,* XI, 191.
38. Esth. 1:12; cf. 2:1; 7:7,10.
39. Prov. 16:14; 20:2.
40. Prov. 12:16; cf. 14:29; 16:32.
41. Prov. 14:17.
42. Deut. 7:13; 11:14; 14:23; Prov. 3:9-10.
43. Gen. 14:18; 27:28; John 2:3,9-10.
44. Num. 15:5,7; 28:14.
45. Num. 18:12; Deut. 18:4.
46. Ps. 104:15; Eccles. 10:19.
47. Eccles. 2:3; Isa. 56:12.
48. 1 Tim. 5:23.
49. Prov. 20:1; 23:29-30; Gen. 9:20-24.
50. Isa. 5:11,22.
51. Prov. 23:20; 1 Tim. 3:8; 5:23; Titus 2:3.
52. Rom. 14:21.
53. 1 Cor. 6:12; 10:23.
54. Ezek. 44:21.
55. Num. 6:4; Judg. 13:7; Amos 2:12.
56. Luke 1:15.
57. Eph. 5:18.
58. 2 Cor. 5:9.
59. Prov. 11:14; 15:22.
60. Job 12:20.
61. John 16:7.

62. Esth. 1:19; 8:8; cf. Dan. 6:8.
63. Herodotus, *History,* VIII, 98.
64. Phil. 4:9.
65. Eph. 5:18; Gal. 5:22-23.
66. 1 Cor. 2:8; Heb. 12:2.

Chapter 2 — God is working his purposes out

1. *Aggadat Esther, 2:1.*
2. Aeschylus, *Pers.* 467ff; Juvenal, *Satires,* X, 174ff; Herodotus, *History,* VII, 3ff; IX, 108ff.
3. Herodotus, *The Histories,* pp.452-3.
4. Rom. 9:5,18; cf. Ps. 2:1-6.
5. Ps. 100:5; Eph. 1:11.
6. Rom. 11:36.
7. Matt. 28:18.
8. Prov. 16:1,9,33.
9. 1 Cor. 13:12.
10. Rom. 8:28.
11. Gen. 45:8.
12. Esth. 1:10,19,21; cf. 2:9.
13. Herodotus, *History,* III, 84.
14. Isa. 45:1.
15. Prov. 21:1.
16. Josephus, *Antiquities,* II. 205.
17. *Megillah,* 15a.
18. Prov. 31:30.
19. Isa. 41:19; 55:13; cf. Zech. 1:8.
20. Dan. 1:7; 2 Kings 24:17; 2 Chr. 36:4.
21. Five men bear the name of Kish in the Old Testament. Like the first Kish (the father of Saul) mentioned in 1 Samuel 9:1, Mordecai's great-grandfather was also a Benjamite. However, we know nothing more of him.
22. Ps. 139:13.
23. Rom. 12:2.
24. Matt. 26:42; Heb. 10:7,9.
25. 1 Peter 3:4.
26. Gen. 39:20-21.
27. Dan. 1:9.
28. Neh. 1:11; 2:1-6.
29. Prov. 1:8-9; 15:5.
30. Phil. 4:22.
31. Xenophon, *Cyropaedia,* VIII. 2,6; Herodotus, *History,* III.120.
32. E.g. Deut. 21:19; 2 Sam. 19:8; Ruth 4:1,11.
33. Cf. Exod. 18:14; Ruth 4:2.
34. Ps. 16:8.
35. John 5:17.
36. Acts 20:28
37. Rom. 8:28.

Chapter 3 — Right behaviour and persecution

1. Exod. 17:16; cf. Num. 24:20; Deut. 25:17-19.
2. Judg. 3:13; 5:14; 6:3,33; 7:12; 10:12; 1 Sam. 27:8; 30:13-18.
3. 2 Sam. 1:8,10.
4. 1 Chr. 4:43.
5. Eccles. 9:11.
6. Matt. 5:16.
7. Matt. 5:43-48.
8. Matt. 7:20.
9. Eccles. 12:13.
10. Ps. 34:9-10; cf. 5:7; 15:4; 22:23; 33:18.
11. Neh. 5:9,15.
12. Ps. 128:1.
13. Exod. 20:20; cf. Gen. 20:11.
14. Job 28:28; Ps. 111:10; Prov. 9:10.
15. Ps. 34:11-14.
16. Exod. 20:3-5.
17. Prov. 17:28; Eccles. 3:7.
18. Acts 4:19.
19. Exod. 20:13.
20. 1 Peter 2:20.
21. 2 Tim. 3:12.
22. Josh. 14:1-2.
23. Prov. 6:16-19; cf. Esth. 3:6,8,13; 5:11.
24. Smerdis the Magus was the son of Cyrus the Great of Persia and the brother of King Cambyses II, who reigned from 529 to 522 B.C. According to both the Greek historian Herodotus and the Persian king Darius' account in an inscription, Smerdis was murdered by his brother, the king, on suspicion of disloyalty, but was later successfully impersonated by Gaumata, a Magus who seized the throne when King Cambyses II died in 522 B.C. He reigned for only eight months, however, before he was slain by Darius and other Persian nobles suspicious of his origin. Some contemporary historians consider that Darius, who succeeded to the throne, invented the story of Gaumata's false claims to justify his actions and that the murdered king was a genuine son of Cyrus (See J. B. Bury, *History of Greece,* Macmillan, 1904, p.234f.).
25. Col. 1:13; 1 Peter 2:9.
26. Matt. 22:21.
27. John 15:18-19.
28. 1 Thess. 4:1-5; 1 Peter 4:3- 4.
29. 1 Peter 3:15.
30. Phil. 2:15.
31. John 16:33.
32. Gen. 3:15.
33. John 8:44.
34. Prov. 29:11.
35. Matt. 12:24.
36. 1 John 4:4.
37. Esth. 8:1; 9:10,24.

38. Cf. Gen. 41:42.
39. Esth. 1:22; 8:9; Dan. 3:4-7.
40. Exod. 12:6.
41. Dr David Barrett, editor of *World Christian Encyclopaedia*, quoted in *Evangelical Times*, December 1987.
42. Eccles. 1:9.
43. Eph. 6:12.
44. Heb. 13:18.

Chapter 4 — The secret of courage
1. 1 Cor. 10:13.
2. Jonah 3:4-9.
3. John Calvin, *Institutes of the Christian Religion,* 1.17.4, The Library of Christian Classics, trans. Ford Lewis Battles, p.216.
4. Eph. 6:10-18.
5. Esth. 4:11; 5:2 (twice); 8:4.
6. Herodotus, *History,* I, 99; III, 72, 77, 84, 118, 140.
7. Prov. 25:6-7.
8. Matt. 11:28-30.
9. Heb. 10:19-22; James 4:8.
10. Rom. 5:1-2; Eph. 2:17-18; 1 Peter 3:18.
11. James 5:17.
12. Eph. 3:20.
13. Acts 4:23-31.
14. Deut. 26:15; 1 Kings 8:30; Neh. 9:27-28; Ps. 57:3.
15. Zech. 2:13.
16. Ps. 33:16-19.
17. Ps. 124:8.
18. Josephus, *Antiquities,* XI, p.227.
19. Ps. 121:4.
20. Cf. Joel 2:32; Matt. 26:24; Acts 2:23; 3:18-19.
21. E.g. Judg. 5:23.
22. Prov. 16:4,9.
23. Matt. 16:25.
24. Prov. 27:6.
25. Gal. 2:11.
26. Luke 22:42.
27. Col. 1:24.
28. Rom. 14:9; 2 Cor. 5:15.
29. John Wesley in his *Commentary on the Bible,* Zondervan, p.255.
30. Gal. 4:4.
31. Rom. 12:2.
32. Eph. 2:10.
33. Lev. 23:27,29,32.
34. 1 Kings 21:9.
35. Neh. 1:4.
36. 2 Sam. 12:22.
37. Dan. 6:18; Ezra 10:6.

38. Joel 1:14.
39. Matt. 9:14; Mark 2:18; Luke 5:33.
40. Matt. 4:2.
41. Matt. 6:16-18.
42. Luke 18:12.
43. Matt. 9:15-17; Mark 2:19-22; Luke 5:34-39.
44. Acts 13:2-3; 14:23.
45. John Calvin, *Commentary on Jeremiah,* vol. 1. p.348. Quoted in Graham Miller, *Calvin's Wisdom*, Banner of Truth, 1992, p.113.
46. H. E. Hopkins, *Charles Simeon of Cambridge*, Hodder & Stoughton, 1977, p.157.
47. Faith Cook, *Samuel Rutherford and his friends*, p.39, quoting from *Letters of Samuel Rutherford,* Bonar Edition 1891, republished by the Banner of Truth Trust, 1984, p.85.
48. Alexander Haldane, *The Lives of Robert and James Haldane*, Banner of Truth edition, 1990, p.670.
49. Ps. 118:9; cf. 146:3,5-9.
50. Deut. 4:30-31.
51. Isa. 40:31.
52. Luke 22:43.
53. 2 Tim. 1:7.
54. Cf. Josh. 1:6,7,9.
55. Esth. 1:3,5,8,9; 2:18; 5:4-5,8,12; 6:14; 7:8; 8:17; 9:17-19,22.
56. Esth. 4:3,15-17.
57. Cf. Ps. 139:16; Jer. 1:5.

Chapter 5 — The way up and the way down
1. Matt. 4:6; Ps. 91:11-12.
2. Ps. 31:15.
3. Herodotus: *The Histories*, p.461.
4. As above, p.452ff.
5. Ps. 132:18.
6. Luke 23:46.
7. James 3:17.
8. James 1:2-8.
9. Isa. 28:29.
10. Prov. 16:15.
11. Mark 6:23.
12. Eph. 3:20.
13. Compare Ezra 7:27; Prov. 16:1.
14. Prov. 26:12; cf. 4:23; 16:5,18.
15. Cf. Prov. 21:24.
16. Roy Plomley, *Desert Island Discs*, Fontana/Collins, 1977, p.27.
17. 1 John 2:16.
18. James 3:5-6.
19. Prov. 16:18.
20. Prov. 13:21.
21. Prov. 27:6.

22. Cf. Ps. 37:12; Prov. 27:4.
23. James 4:6.
24. Phil. 2:5-8.
25. Cf. Phil. 2:19-22.
26. Eph. 1:20-21.

Chapter 6 — God's perfect timing
1. Cf. Ps. 34:15-16.
2. Ps. 135:14.
3. Ps. 43:1.
4. Rom. 12:19.
5. Richard Sibbes, *Works,* Banner of Truth edition, 1973, vol. I, p.206f.
6. Herodotus, *History,* III, 139-41,153; V, 11; VIII, 85,90; IX, 107.
7. Mal. 3:16.
8. Matt. 25:34-40.
9. Cf. Gen. 41:42; 1 Sam. 18:4.
10. Cf. Gen. 41:43.
11. Ps. 124:7-8.
12. Prov. 10:28; cf. 22:11,29.
13. Rom. 8:32.
14. Jer. 10:23.
15. 1 Peter 5:5.
16. Others before them had made the same observation (cf. Num. 22-24; Dan. 2:46-47; 3:28-29).
17. Ps. 83:3-4.
18. Acts 4:24-30.
19. Tony Lambert, *China's Christian Millions*, Monarch, 1999, p.9.
20. Matt. 16:18.
21. Rom. 8:31.
22. Gen. 15:8.
23. Luke 18:7.
24. Matt. 14:23-25.
25. John 11:6.
26. E.g. Ps. 13:1; 74:9-11.
27. E.g. Isa. 49:23; Rev. 3:9.

Chapter 7 — This is the day
1. Ps. 73:16-17.
2. Isa. 27:2-3.
3. Isa. 49:15.
4. Gen. 19:3; 26:30; 2 Sam. 3:20.
5. Gen. 29:22: Judg. 14:10.
6. Prov. 25:15.
7. Cf. Judg. 2:14; 3:8; 4:2; 10:7.
8. Cf. Acts 5:1-11.
9. Gal. 4:4,5; cf. Titus 2:11.
10. Rom. 1:4.
11. Eccles. 12:14.

12. The New King James Version.
13. Prov. 14:35.
14. Prov. 11:8; 12:13, 26:27; cf. Eccles. 10:8.
15. Ps. 73:18-20.
16. Job 5:13.
17. James 2:13.
18. 1 Cor. 4:5.
19. 2 Thess. 1:8-9; Rev. 20:11-15.
20. Prov. 13:22.
21. Matt. 7:2.
22. Rev. 14:13.
23. Cf. 1 Sam. 4:19.
24. Rom. 9:1-3.
25. John 19:22.
26. Cf. Esth. 6:10; 9:29,31; 10:3.
27. Ps. 118:24,25.
28. Mark 10:29-30.

Chapter 8 — Tables turned!
1. The Jews' 'language' must have been Hebrew, the language of Judah (Neh. 13:24; 2 Kings 18:26,28; Isa. 36:11,13).
2. Prov. 11:10-11.
3. 2 Sam. 22:29; Job 18:5-6.
4. Cf. Ps. 36:9; 97:11; 112:4; 139:12.
5. 2 Sam. 23:3-4.
6. Zech. 8:20-23; cf. Ps. 18:43-44.
7. Isa. 14:1; cf. Prov. 28:12; 16:7.
8. Heb. 2:9.
9. 1 Peter 1:8-9.
10. 1 John 3:2.
11. Cf., e.g., Josh. 8:29; 1 Sam. 31:10.
12. Luke 19:41-42.
13. Gen. 14:22-23.
14. 1 Sam. 15.
15. Col. 3:5.
16. Matt. 13:22.
17. Col. 3:1-4.

Chapter 9
1. Neh. 8:10.
2. When the Israelites were being invaded annually by the Midianites, they expressed this cry (Judg. 6:6-7).
3. Gen. 41:40.
4. Dan. 5:29.
5. 1 Cor. 11:23-25.
6. Acts 20:7.
7. 1 Cor. 16:2; Rev. 1:10.
8. Exod. 20:11; cf. 15:13; Deut. 5:15.

9. Mark 6:31
10. Acts 2:42.
11. Acts 2:46.
12. Exod. 16:3.
13. Exod. 12:14-17.
14. Ps. 103:2.
15. 2 Peter 1:12-13,15; 3:1-2; Jude 5,17, etc.
16. 1 Cor. 5:8.
17. Carol Armitage, *Reaching for the Goal*, OMF, 1993, p.40.